MW01590917

The Loire

Intelligent Guides to Wines & Top Vineyards

Benjamin Lewin MW

Copyright © 2015, 2016 Benjamin Lewin

Update September 2016

Vendange Press

www.vendangepress.com

Preface

Based on my book, *Wines of France*, this Guide is devoted specifically to the Loire, extending from Muscadet, through Anjou and Touraine, to Sancerre and its surrounding appellations. The first part discusses each part of the region and its wines; the second part has individual profiles of the top producers. The basic idea is that the first part explains the character and range of the wines, and the second part shows how each winemaker interprets that character.

In the first part I address the nature of the wines made today and ask how this has changed, how it's driven by tradition or competition, and how styles may evolve in the future. I show how the wines are related to the terroir and to the types of grape varieties that are grown, and I explain the classification system. For each region, I suggest reference wines that I believe typify the area; in some cases, where there is a split between, for example, modernists and traditionalists, there may be wines from each camp.

There's no single definition for what constitutes a top producer. Leading producers range from those who are so prominent as to represent the common public face of an appellation to those who demonstrate an unexpected potential on a tiny scale. The producers profiled in the guide should represent the best of both tradition and innovation in wine in the region

In the profiles, I have tried to give a sense of each producer's aims for his wines, of the personality and philosophy behind them—to meet the person who makes the wine, as it were, as much as to review the wines themselves. For each producer I suggest reference wines that are a good starting point for understanding his style. Most of the producers welcome visits, although some require appointments: details are in the profiles.

The guide is based on many visits to France over recent years. I owe an enormous debt to the hundreds of producers who cooperated in this venture by engaging in discussion and opening innumerable bottles for tasting. This guide would not have been possible without them.

Benjamin Lewin MW

How to read the producer profiles

The second part of this guide consists of profiles of individual wine producers. Each profile shows a sample label, a picture of the winery, and details of production, followed by a description of the producer and winemaker. The producer's rating (from one to four stars) is shown to the right of the name.

The profiles are organized geographically, and each group of profiles is preceded by a map showing the locations of starred producers to help plan itineraries.

A full list of the symbols used in the profiles appears at the start of the profile section. This is an example of a profile:

Hospices de Beaune

Hospices de Beaune

VOLNAY
Premier Cru
Appellation Volnay Contrôlée
Cuvée Blondeau
ॐ
Mis en bouteille par
Jean-Luc Aegerter
Négociant-Eleveur à 21700 Nuits-Saint-Georges

13 % vol.　　　　　Produit de France　　750 ml

Hotel Dieu, Beaune, France
address

03 80 24 44 02

Catherine Guillemot

@ catherine.guillemot@ch-beaune.fr

Corton *principal AOP*

Beaune 1er, Nicolas Rolin
red reference wine

Corton Charlemagne, Charlotte Dumay
white reference wine

www.hospices-de-beaune.com

details of producer
60 ha; 400,000 bottles
vineyards & production

The Hospices de Beaune was founded in 1443 by Nicolas Rolin, chancellor of Burgundy, as a hospital for the poor. Standing in the heart of Beaune, the original buildings of the Hotel Dieu, now converted into a museum, surround a courtyard where an annual auction of wines was first held in 1859. The wines come from vineyards held as part of the endowment of the Hospices, and are sold in November to negociants who then take possession of the barrels and mature the wines in their own styles. (Today the auction is held in the modern covered marketplace opposite the Hotel Dieu.) There are 45 cuvées (32 red and 13 white); most come from premier or grand crus from the Côte de Beaune or Côte de Nuits, but because holdings are small (depending on past donations of land to the Hospices) many cuvées consist of blends from different crus (and are identified by brand names). The vines are cultivated, and the wine is made, by the Hospices. For some years the vineyards of the Hospices were not tended as carefully as they might have been, and the winemaking was less than perfect, but the appointment of a new régisseur has led to improvements in the present century. The name of the Hospices is only a starting point, because each negociant stamps his own style on the barriques he buys.

Contents

The Loire

"Loire producers are thought of as traditionally making white wine, but now there is some red wine," says François Robin of the producers' organization, Inter-Loire, but this is somewhat of an understatement as production today splits more equally between red, white, and rosé. The emphasis is on cool climate varieties, as the Loire is at the northern limit for viticulture; in fact, it is only due to the ameliorating influence of the river that wine can be made at all in the region.

The longest river in France, the Loire runs more or less north to Sancerre, where it turns west. No longer navigable, it meanders through the wine regions for about 400 km (250 miles) before it empties out into the Atlantic. The Loire is divided into four general regions for wine production: the Nantais near the coast, Anjou centered on Angers, Touraine centered on Tours, and the Centre around Sancerre. All styles of wine are found in the Loire as a whole, but going from west to east, the Nantais is dominated by dry white, the largest production in Anjou is rosé, the bulk of Touraine is red, and the Centre (the general name of the eastern vineyards) focuses on dry whites. The sweet whites of Anjou and Touraine have a great reputation, although production volume is small.

The wine regions of the Loire are near the river or its tributaries. Legend holds that vines were being cultivated on the banks of the Loire before the Roman invasion of Gaul. Whether or not this is true, there are detailed descriptions of winegrowing by the sixth century, and by the Middle Ages the forests along the river were being cleared to plant vineyards. Planting was confined to the area immediately around the rivers, not because this was the most appropriate terroir, but because it made it possible to transport the wine to market. During the twelfth to fifteenth centuries the wines were drunk at the Royal Court in the Loire and exported to England.

Before the phylloxera epidemic in the nineteenth century, there were about 160,000 ha of vines along the Loire. Now there are about 50,000 ha in the four regions devoted to AOP wines and another 20,000 in IGP. The regional description of IGP Val de Loire covers the whole area and accounts for almost all the IGP wine (this used to be the Vin de Pays du Jardin de la France). Vineyards lie

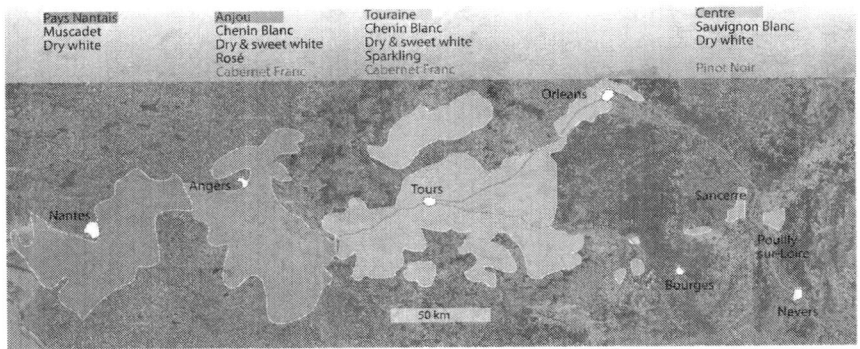

Pays Nantais	Anjou	Touraine	Centre
Muscadet	Chenin Blanc	Chenin Blanc	Sauvignon Blanc
Dry white	Dry & sweet white	Dry & sweet white	Dry white
	Rosé	Sparkling	
	Cabernet Franc	Cabernet Franc	Pinot Noir

Extending for several hundred kilometers, the Loire contains four distinct wine-producing regions.

mostly on the south side of the river. Although the region is protected from climatic extremes, its cool climate ensures good acidity for the whites. Ripening can be a problem for the reds.

Each of the four regions of the Loire has its own character and focus. The white wines are mostly varietal-based, with the variety changing from west to east: Muscadet in the Nantais, Chenin Blanc in Anjou and Touraine, and Sauvignon Blanc in Sancerre or Pouilly Fumé. With such diversity of varieties, you might not expect to see much universality of style, but the cool climate is reflected in the common features of crisp, fresh fruits for both reds and whites.

Almost half the production of the Loire today is dry white wine. Muscadet is more than half of the total white. Melon de Bourgogne is the formal name for the grape variety, but today it is more often just called Muscadet. The most planted white grape in the Loire, Muscadet accounts for almost all production in the Nantais.

In Anjou and Touraine, production is more or less evenly divided between red, rosé, and white (including still and sparkling). White and sparkling wines are dominated by Chenin Blanc, the oldest white grape of the region. Chenin Blanc is made in a complete range of styles, from dry to sweet, and from still to sparkling. The relative proportions of still and sparkling wine depend on the weather. In better vintages, more still wine is made; in less successful vintages, more is turned into sparkling wine. Production of sweet wines also depends greatly on vintage, in particular whether the growing season extends long enough into autumn for a late harvest.

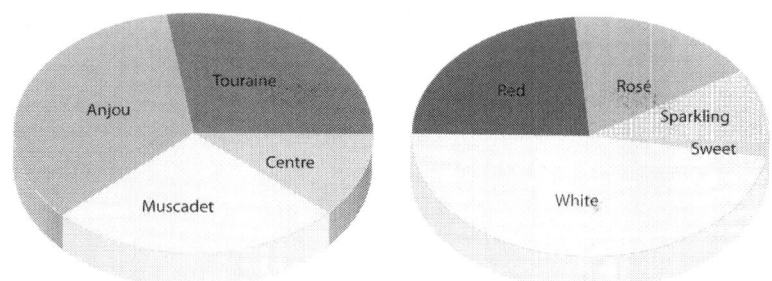

The major production of the Loire is split between Muscadet, Anjou, and Touraine, with less in the Centre. Almost half is dry white, and most of the rest is red or rosé.

Rosé dominates the production of Anjou. The largest single category is the slightly sweet Cabernet d'Anjou, which usually comes mostly from Cabernet Franc. Rosé can be made in most of the appellations of Anjou and Touraine, but no individual area is considered a quality leader. Production of the generic Rosé d'Anjou, which can be made anywhere in the region, has declined.

Red wine is most important in Touraine (where it is about half of all production), but the red wine areas extend over the border into Anjou. There is a blur in focus between the regions, as the red wines are more similar than different. Cabernet Franc is the major black grape of both Anjou and Touraine. It came from Bordeaux; in 1635, "Cardinal Richelieu sent several thousands of the best vine of Bordeaux to the Abbé Breton in Chinon." Still known as Breton or Petit Breton in the Loire, this was Cabernet Franc. Most red wines are pure varietals. A small amount of Cabernet Sauvignon is also grown (less than 10% of the amount of Cabernet Franc), but is limited to a small proportion, or even disallowed, in some appellations.

Entry level Cabernet Franc is vastly improved from a generation ago, showing light, fresh fruits with no trace of the vegetative notes that used to mark unripe Cabernet. This is great progress, but the problem for me is that the price of mastering the tannins and avoiding herbaceousness is that while the wine is not exactly eviscerated, it has lost the typicity of Cabernet Franc. Fruitier, more vibrant wine can be better made at this level from lesser varieties.

It's back to white wine at the eastern end of the Loire wine regions, where Sauvignon Blanc dominates Sancerre and the other appellations of the Centre (so called because the area is central in France). Sauvignon Blanc probably originated in the Loire, and may be an offspring of Savagnin, the white grape of the Jura. It became the dominant variety during the replanting that followed phylloxera, but recently Pinot Noir has been making a comeback in Sancerre.

All over the Loire, the style of the white wine has been modernized by a move to greater ripeness. Muscadet now shows a tendency to emphasize fruits rather than minerality. In Anjou and Touraine, Chenin Blanc has lost its characteristic "wet wool" in favor of more direct fruits. In Sancerre and Pouilly Fumé, Sauvignon Blanc is less aggressive, with its former grassy or even herbaceous flavors replaced by citrus fruits, sometimes merging with stone fruits. Perhaps it's a little harsh to say that there's a tendency to reduce intensity in favor of amorphous fruit flavors, but it might be fair to say that there's a certain sense of convergence among entry-level wines, and in order to see real regional and varietal character it's necessary to seek out specific cuvées.

A significant change is an emerging focus by producers all over the Loire on expressing single cépages through a variety of terroirs. Traditionally most producers used to make an assemblage for a single wine, or possibly a couple of cuvées, from their various plots. Voicing a common view, "At first I worked to select lots and assemble them, but things have advanced, today there is much more focus on terroir," François Pinon says in Vouvray. In each region the top producers now often offer several cuvées, each representing a different terroir.

One point to be made is the sheer value of the top dry white or red wines from the Loire. It would be hard to find a white Burgundy or red Bordeaux of equivalent quality at the same price level. With the modernization of style in the past decade, these can be wines with significant interest as well as an attractive price. The top sweet wines are priced more highly.

Muscadet

Winegrowers in Muscadet have a sense that the region is in free fall. Since 2000, the area of AOP vineyards has halved from 17,500 ha to 9,000 ha. The number of producers has fallen as wine production has simply become uneconomic, especially after a frost destroyed a large part of the crop in 2008. Today there are about 600 producers left. An incidental benefit has been a move towards quality. "It's a good thing that vineyards have been reduced, it's let us concentrate on the better terroirs," says Marie-Luce Métaireau of Domaine du Grand Mouton. "13,000 ha is too much," says Michel Brégeon. "It's necessary to select the best terroirs and to create village appellations with a new hierarchy."

The myth about the origins of Muscadet is that Melon de Bourgogne was imported into the Nantais in the early eighteenth century, when growers were looking for a grape variety to replace the black varieties that had been killed by frost in the great winter freeze of 1709. But in fact Melon was already an abundant variety a century earlier. At all events, by the eighteenth century, the Nantais had switched to white wine production. During this period, much of the wine was exported by Dutch traders from the port of Nantes after distillation into eau de vie; the thin, acid wines of the region were ideal for this purpose. Another grape giving good results was Folle Blanche, today one of the principal varieties for brandy production in Cognac and Armagnac. It's known in the Loire as Gros Plant because of the large size of its grapes. This became the most widely planted variety.

When phylloxera struck, plantings were two thirds Gros Plant. During the twentieth century, the balance shifted to producing white wine for drinking, and Muscadet (Melon) increased to become the vast majority. Gros Plant was a VDQS (a level below AOC) until 2011, but became an IGP when the rules changed. Production has dropped steadily to less than ten per cent of Muscadet. It its own appellation, Gros Plant Nantais.

The alternative to producing Muscadet is to plant other varieties under the IGP Val de Loire. François Lieubeau is a leader, with one quarter of total 80 ha planted to IGP, mostly for Chardonnay and Sauvignon Blanc. Prices are similar to entry-level Muscadet, but because yields are higher, the IGP is more profitable. Is the IGP more modern? "Muscadet is drunk by old fashioned people," says François. "If you say Val de Loire Chardonnay or Sauvignon Blanc, it's very effective, but that's not the case for Muscadet, it's hard to be competitive."

The Muscadet appellation includes a hierarchy of sub-appellations). Muscadet describes the entire area where Melon de

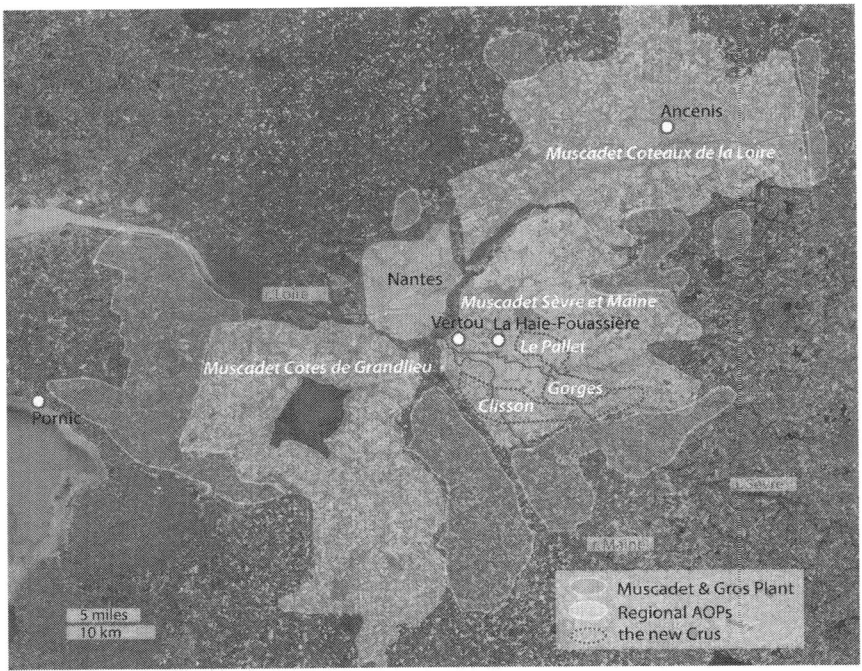

The Muscadet region forms a semi circle around Nantes and is divided into regional appellations. Le Pallet, Gorges, and Clisson are the first three Cru Communaux.

Bourgogne is produced. The most important AOP is Muscadet Sèvre et Maine, which has about 80% of the total plantings. (Sèvre and Maine are the two major rivers that run through the region; they are tributaries joining the Loire at Nantes.) To the west is Muscadet Côtes de Grandlieu and to the northeast is Muscadet Coteaux de la Loire. But the most important determinant of quality is a feature of production called *sur lie*. This describes the tradition of keeping the wine on the lees through the winter, and then bottling directly in the spring. The wine gains additional flavor and texture from its contact with the lees; sometimes just a faint touch of spritzen from carbon dioxide remains at the time of bottling.

About half of Muscadet Sèvre et Maine is bottled sur lie. One restriction is that the wine must be bottled no later than November of the year following the harvest; originally intended as a marker for quality, this can now be counter-productive, as producers who want to use longer lees aging cannot label the wine as sur lie.

Changing Styles in Muscadet

Muscadet has responded to the market with a change of style at the generic level, emphasizing fruit and aromatics; these wines are direct in flavor but well made, often with an initial slightly perfumed or aromatic impression, which persists through the palate. I have never really considered Muscadet as an aromatic variety, but in these wines, you see phenolics as much as flavor. They remain quite acidic and low in alcohol, but otherwise fit the image of a modern wine better than a traditional Muscadet. They can be somewhat interdenominational, and although they retain acidity, I do not think they will complement oysters in the same way as a more saline or savory traditional Muscadet. The problem here is lack of typicity: nothing distinguishes these wines, except perhaps price, from the competition.

Muscadet passed through a period when producers went to extremes of vinification in order to try to develop character, such as using new oak or performing malolactic fermentation. This has mostly died out now. These wines can be interesting, but blur the focus, and sometimes I feel they are not what I look for in Muscadet, especially when new oak is used. My own view is that the wines develop more interest as the result of lees aging than they do from exposure to new oak; I do not really think the grape variety is fat enough to support the oak. Wines with long lees aging are a better way to make the point that Muscadet has potential for producing wine that is interesting as it ages.

A major, and controversial, determinant of style is battonage—stirring up the wine while it is on the lees. Producers use more battonage if they are looking for a more powerful style, and less battonage if they are looking for elegance. The combination of longer lees aging and battonage adds stone fruit flavors to the citrus fruits. The wine can become quite complex, but not everyone wants to see the increased richness. "We want the wine to be natural and fresh; battonage introduces richness, which is very nice, but is not our style here," says Marie-Luce Métaireau, explaining why Domaine du Grand Mouton does not use battonage. The traditional view of Muscadet is that it should be drunk right away, while it is fresh. However, minerality begins to show around two years of age. "Few people know this aspect of Muscadet because they drink the wine soon after the vintage," says Patrick Macé, winemaker at Chéreau Carré. Focusing on youthfulness definitely gives a mistaken view of the better cuvées or crus, where it takes at least four or five years for the increasing complexity with age to develop. Marie-Luce Métaireau at Domaine du Grand Mouton recollects that in the fifties and sixties, her father used to say that Muscadet would age well, but when he took old Muscadet to wine fairs in the area, people did not want to taste it. "It's only in the past 15 years or so that people have accepted the idea of older vintages from Muscadet," she says. The most impressive demonstration of aging came from a tasting at Domaine Luneau-Papin, where young wines show a nice sense of restrained minerality, and become more savory and herbal with age. The top wines have significant potential for aging; the oldest I tasted were almost fifteen years old, and still lively.

But only a relatively small proportion of Muscadet is made by independent growers. More than two thirds is produced by negociants. "There used to be about twenty negociant houses in the Nantais but the larger negociants have purchased most of them and now most Muscadet is made by only two or three negociants," says François Robin. The problem here is the lack of local commitment: Muscadet becomes just one possible source for supply of cheap white wine. Muscadet Sèvre et Maine sur lie bottled by a grower committed to quality can be fresh and attractive—perhaps not a competitor to Sancerre or Chablis, but nonetheless a refreshing accompaniment to sea food. Many of the negociants' wines are somewhat characterless. "The big negociants who sell in bulk have spoiled everything. The wine is made without any passion, all sorts of treatments are used," says Guy Bossard. The only good side to this is increased pressure for growers to bottle their own wine. "Negociants are less interested in Muscadet; they prefer to buy wines from Spain and the south of France, and this is pushing growers who want to stay in business to produce their own wine," says Marie Chartier-Luneau. "For whatever reason, there's never been much interest in cooperatives, so it's either sell to a negociant or do it all yourself," she adds.

Introducing Crus in Muscadet

The attempt to lift Muscadet out of the doldrums focuses on the introduction of Crus Communaux (Communal Crus): anywhere else these would probably simply be called premier crus. They identify the best terroirs in Muscadet Sèvre et Maine, and have higher standards for vinification. The first three were approved in 2011, another four are expected to be approved soon, and two more are still being studied. Yields are lower in the crus, and the wine spends longer on the lees. The minimum of two years on the less in Gorges and Clisson, for example, means that wine cannot be labeled as "sur lie," because it cannot be bottled by the limit in the Muscadet regulations. The extension of lees contact beyond this period makes for more intense wines (and also means there will not be any spritzen remaining at bottling). Definition of the crus is partly a recognition of existing practices. "The great variety of subsoils in Muscadet has been little known; we are working to define the geography, which is the basis for the crus. But for a number of years the vignerons have been treating wines from different terroirs separately," explains François Robin. In fact, the names of the crus have been used on labels for some years, often appearing more prominently than "Muscadet."

The intention is to emphasize variety. "Historically Muscadet was very well known, but considered always to have the single characteristic of freshness. It's difficult today to make people understand that it's not just one homogeneous wine, but comes from a diversity of terroirs, and has evolved in quality to a range extending from the regional wines to the communal crus. Our job is to explain to people that Muscadet is no longer just a single wine, but that it can age well. We would like people to forget their past impressions of Muscadet and be surprised by the crus. We want to put an 's' on Muscadet and make it plural," says François Robin. "Sometimes people say, 'this is good but it's not Muscadet'," he adds.

My own experience has been that the crus show more intensity of flavor, but generally follow the same stylistic imperatives as

Muscadet has expanses of vineyards overlooked by small villages, with the church spires often visible on the horizon.

Muscadet Sèvre et Maine. Applied to wines coming from better terroirs, lower yields and longer periods for maturation (typically eighteen months or more on the lees) definitely pay off in superior quality, but I would say that the style is not very different. What you get with Muscadet where there has been extensive lees aging is a sense of structure, showing as a sort of granular texture to the palate. When the wine has been aged in stainless steel, this offers a counterpoise against its natural freshness. When barriques are used, they are usually old enough for the wood influence to be simply oxidative rather than to add any oak flavors, and there may be a softer impression, even extending to a faint sensation of nuttiness (especially when lees aging has been very long). Usually Muscadet AOPs are aged in stainless steel, but the crus tend to be aged in old barriques.

The other direction is to emphasize differences in terroir. Muscadet has quite varied terroirs, mostly derived from types of metamorphic rocks. The most common are gneiss, orthogneiss, and granite, but serpentine, amphibolite, and gabbro (a type of basalt) are also found. The crus epitomize the variation: Clisson has a mix

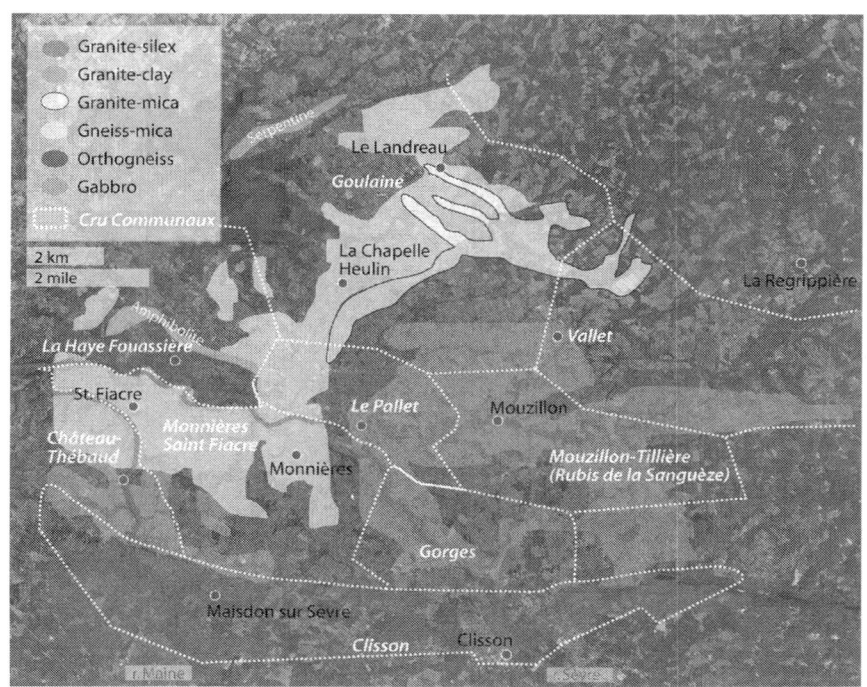

The crus (and proposed crus) have different geologies. Existing crus are Gorges, Clisson, and Le Pallet; Goulaine, Monnières et Saint-Fiacre, Château-Thébaud, Mouzillon-Tillères are expected to be approved shortly. Different types of granite are dominant in Clisson and Château-Thébaud; gabbro is dominant in Gorges and Mouzillon-Tillière (also known as Rubis de la Sanguèze as rubis is the local name for gabbro); schist features in Goulaine (with mica in both granite and gneiss); there is gneiss with some orthogneiss in Monnières Saint Fiacre; and Le Pallet has various soil types.

of pebbles and granite, Gorge extends across the river Sèvre with soils from gabbro to clay and quartz, Le Pallet is a warm spot (harvest is usually early here) with gneiss and gabbro, and Château-Thébaud is based on granite.

Moving away from the tradition of making an assemblage to get regularity in the wine, top producers now tend to make cuvées from parcels to emphasize terroir. "I think we have 20-30 producers who are looking for terroir in their wines. I think this is the richness of Muscadet, the future is to make different wines," says Marie Chartier-Luneau at Domaine Luneau-Papin, where eight different

*A steep cliff rising up from the Maine river shows the typical granite terroir
with thin topsoil of Château-Thébaud.*

cuvées, distinguished by terroir and vine age, offer interesting inter-
plays of savory notes against a background of fruits that changes
with the terroir and the age of the vines.

The most brilliant demonstration of terroir came from a tasting
at Domaine de l'Ecu, where Guy Bossard was a pioneer in expressing terroir in Muscadet. "At first we looked for complexity by
assemblage and I continue to do that; but the best tasters in my clientele are looking for a personality, an expression of the terroir. I
started with my father, we always vinified each parcel separately,
and the assemblage was done at bottling. We started to bottle the
separate terroirs around 1970," he says. "The cépage is the same,
the vintage is the same, the work in the vines is the same, the work
to make the wine is the same, so if we see differences in the wines it
must be the terroir." The emphasis on terroir extends to labeling the
wines simply by the types of terroir: Gneiss, Orthogneiss, and Granite. The wines become progressively more precise, mineral, and
savory, and a little weightier, moving along the terroirs.

Variations on granite became clear from a tasting at Domaine de la Pépière, where Marc Ollivier and Rémi Branger are regarded as among the leaders in modern Muscadet. "We were making wine from two different parcels of granite, one at Château Thébaud and one just north of it, and we only understood the differences we were finding in the wines when we saw the geological map [which was prepared as part of the development of the crus]. The granite of Clisson is more siliceous, which captures heat better. Château-Thébaud is mostly granite, but it is a specific type, and has more clay," explains Rémi.

Although the crus certainly have distinctive terroirs, there is enough heterogeneity within each cru that it's not obvious at this point whether they will develop distinctive styles related to terroir, or whether the variety of approaches from different producers will mean that there is no single typicity for any one cru. The crus offer the logical extension of the tendency towards longer lees aging for the best wines; as well as showing more intensity and character than simple Muscadet Sèvre et Maine, they also have significantly greater aging potential. They tend to become more mineral as they age. I'm inclined to the view that their importance comes more from providing an easy way to identify the best wines than for specific characters associated with individual crus.

So will the crus rescue Muscadet? They account for only a tiny proportion of the vineyards. "The crus are not made in sufficient quantity to resolve the *crise*, but we think they will be a locomotive; people will see Muscadet in a more positive light," says François Robin. "The Crus are a very good thing because it's important to have wines like that to make people understand that Muscadet is not just for drinking with oysters," says Rémi Branger. The most negative opinion comes from Guy Bossard, who thinks the regulations do not go far enough. "The idea is interesting, but the regulations are not strict enough. You cannot make grand crus with industrial methods. They have not required manual harvest. You need to use natural yeasts," he believes. The issue of harvesting may be a critical point. "To harvest by machine you have to make a higher trellis and you lose the typicity of the wine. Muscadet should be trimmed low and the grapes sheltered under the umbrella of the large leaves," says Marie-Luce Métaireau.

Reference Wines for Muscadet	
Muscadet Sèvre et Maine	Domaine de l'Ecu, Granite Domaine Pierre Luneau-Papin, L de l'Or Domaine du Grand Mouton, Cuvée #1
Muscadet Sèvre et Maine (with MLF and oak)	Château de la Fruitière, M de la Fruitière
Gorges	Michel Brégeon
Le Pallet	Vignerons de Pallet
Clisson	Domaine de la Pépière
Château-Thébaud	Domaine de la Pépière
Monnières St. Fiacre	Domaine La Haute Févrie
Goulaine	Domaine Pierre Luneau-Papin, Excelsior
Gros Plant de Nantais	Domaine Pierre Luneau-Papin

I might not go so far as François Robin, who says that, "In a blind tasting you would find the Crus Communaux to be more like Burgundy than Muscadet," but the Burgundian model certainly holds insofar as there are interesting differences between terroirs that accentuate with age. One great advantage of Muscadet is that it is possibly the only region in France that does not have problems with increasing alcohol. This may partly be due to a propensity to harvest early. Elsewhere in France, the growing season has been lengthened by postponing harvest to get riper berries. But in Muscadet, they are not following the trend; they are more concerned about maintaining freshness as the important criterion. In any case, it's fair to say that there is no risk of alcohol obscuring the terroir. The crus are definitely the way forward, but it remains to be seen whether they (and equivalent cuvées) can have enough impact on the market to change the general perspective of Muscadet.

Anjou

Anjou has the best known appellations in the Loire for dry wines, both red and white, and for sweet (white) dessert wines, although in each category there is a counterpart in Touraine. The most important appellation for red wine is Saumur-Champigny, made exclusively from Cabernet Franc: just to the east are Bourgueil and Chinon in Touraine. The top dry white wines of Anjou come from the small area of Savennières, just outside Angers; the closest competitor in Touraine would be a dry wine from Vouvray. Production is really tiny in the top appellations for sweet wines, Chaume, Quarts de Chaume, and Bonnezeaux, and here the top sweet wines from Vouvray are effective rivals for the crown in the Loire.

Anjou's greatest production by far is rosé. Produced anywhere in Anjou, Cabernet d'Anjou is a slightly sweet rosé, usually made

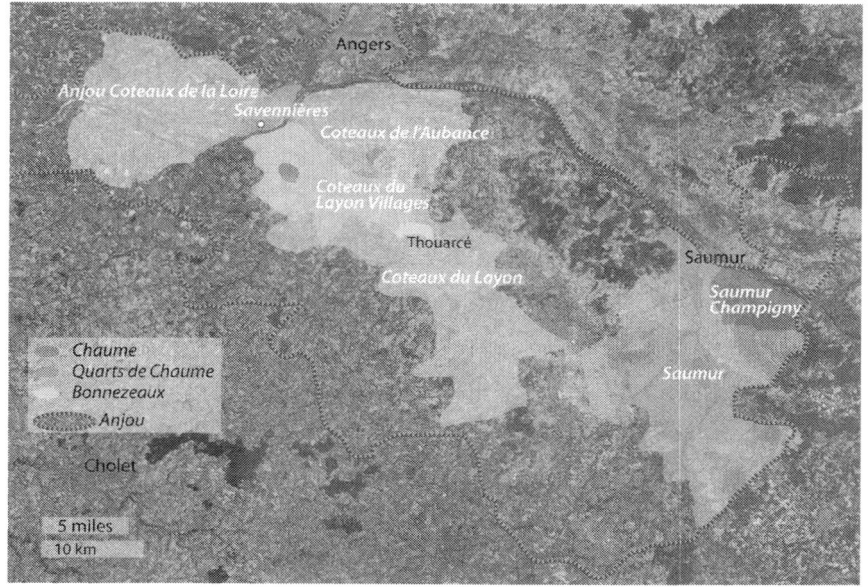

The Anjou region is defined by the Anjou Villages AOP. The western part contains appellations devoted principally to white wine, including the small AOPs for the top sweet wines (see key). Savennières is the top AOP for dry white wine. The eastern part of the region around Saumur produces reds as well as whites. Saumur-Champigny is exclusively red.

from Cabernet Franc (although Cabernet Sauvignon is also allowed). Rosé d'Anjou is not quite as sweet, and can come from any of several black grape varieties. (So can Rosé de Loire, which is dry).

After the rosés, the next most important single appellation in terms of quantity is Saumur Mousseux, the sparkling wine from the large area of Saumur (made from Chenin Blanc, Chardonnay, and Cabernet Franc). Although red comes after rosé in total production, it is divided among many appellations.

All white wine in Anjou and Touraine comes exclusively from Chenin Blanc. Sometimes called Pineau de la Loire locally, it may have originated in Anjou in the ninth century, subsequently migrating to Touraine in the fifteenth. The big issue with Chenin Blanc is always the yield. At low yields, the wine can have character, but at high yields it is completely bland. It has natural high acidity.

Anjou whites tend to show direct fruit flavors, usually in the direction of citrus, sometimes accompanied by a fugitive whiff of exotic fruits. High acidity is common, but necessary to keep the flavor spectrum lively. There can be a touch of superficial richness, which increases further by the time you reach Vouvray and Montlouis in Touraine. This may be partly due to the change in terroir from schist in Anjou to chalk in Touraine, but is probably more a stylistic choice, with a tendency to leave a little residual sugar in the wine in Vouvray.

The New Character of Chenin Blanc

"Chenin is more civilized today, we look for more fruit now," as Jacques Couly of Couly-Dutheil said. The traditional description for the white wines of Anjou and Touraine used to be "wet dog," "wet straw," or "wet wool," according to your predilections, all reflecting a somewhat humid impression of the variety. Perhaps this resulted from incompletely ripe grapes, but it is no longer appropriate. Today I often get a flavor spectrum for Chenin Blanc between cereal and nutty, with a savory, almost earthy edge, accompanied by fruits ranging from citrus to stone, sometimes with a hint of apples. (As Chenin Blanc rarely undergoes malolactic fermentation, there is often enough malic acid to create a faint impression of apples). Some people see quince in the wine.

Does this simply reflects a greater degree of maturity in Chenin Blanc. "Well, harvesting later is one important change, but the move to more natural winemaking, including using native yeasts and using less sulfur is important," says Evelyne de Pontbriand of Domaine du Closel. "But a major factor was that the wine had to be bottled at the latest by the following June, because the cellars are above ground. Being able to bottle later (because of air conditioning) has a big effect. So does the use of barriques, which are made possible because now we can do extended élevage in temperature controlled cellars. So there are multiple factors."

Is there a typical style for Chenin Blanc? The tradition used to be to avoid exposure to oak or malolactic fermentation, giving a decidedly crisp wine. Today maturation in oak is more common. At Château de Fesles, winemaker Gilles Bigot uses a mixture of oak and acacia. "Acacia gives a fruitier and more aromatic impression; it does not give such a woody impression as oak," he explains. Barriques have become common for the top wines, although the proportion of new wood is usually limited. When new barriques are used, most often there is no MLF, so you do not get the pronounced aromas of vanillin and butter that are often associated with combining new oak with MLF. New oak without malolactic fermentation gives an impression more akin to walking into a first year barrel cellar: lots of smoky impressions and that faint sense of fresh-cut oak. While this can be appealing in itself, it isn't necessarily something that melds well with Chenin Blanc. I have had only a few examples of Chenin exposed to large proportions of new oak, and I believe it is usually a mistake.

The "new" typicity of Chenin avoids those humid notes that used to be associated with the variety, but has a slightly savory edge, accentuated by late harvest when there are botrytized grapes. The general tendency in Savennières is becoming quite Burgundian: maturing the entry level wine in cuve, the intermediate wine in old barriques, and perhaps using young barriques, and more extended time on the lees, for the top wine. Some producers have become laissez-faire about malolactic fermentation, which means there can be a change of style from year to year. All this marks a significant change in the past ten or twenty years. "When I was young, Savennières was always semi-dry, and we changed the style at the end of the 1960s. We never used to age on the lees; that started in 2000.

And then we introduced a little MLF. The new generation try to make wine like Burgundy, but we don't have the same soils or cépages. As a result of changes we drink the entry-level wine younger—in the first two years—but the top wines last longer," says Luc Bizard at Château d'Epiré.

Minerality in Savennières

Savennières brings out the savory side of Chenin Blanc. Consisting of three hills facing south-southwest towards the river, Savennières makes the best dry white wines of the Loire (although historically it was known for its sweet or semi-sweet wines). It declined to only 46 planted hectares in 1977, but revived in the 1980s as growers from neighboring sweet wine appellations became interested in producing dry Savennières. Today's wines from Savennières are typically fresh when young, then close up for some years, and finally mature gracefully as the longest lived dry wines of the region. Due to a protected microclimate, Savennières has less rain than Touraine, so the grapes ripen more reliably, and alcohol levels are a little higher. The Savennières AOC was restricted to dry wines until the rules were changed in 1996 to allow sweet wines, but the overwhelming proportion remains dry. You might say that the whites of Chinon and Saumur give a more modern impression than those of Savennières, with more overt fruit—but for that very reason, less typicity of the variety. Savennières tends more to the mineral side.

Savennières is a small appellation, yet carved out within it are two further tiny appellations, Savennières Coulée de Serrant and Savennières Roches-aux- Moines. Curiously these are not premier crus of Savennières, but actually named as independent appellations. This raises the question of what about Coulée de Serrant and Roche-aux-Moines is distinctively different from Savennières? Assessment is complicated by the fact that Coulée de Serrant is a monopole, owned exclusively by Nicolas Joly of Château Roche aux Moines. It's difficult to determine whether the character of a vineyard is due to unique terroir or to winemaking when there is only a single owner.

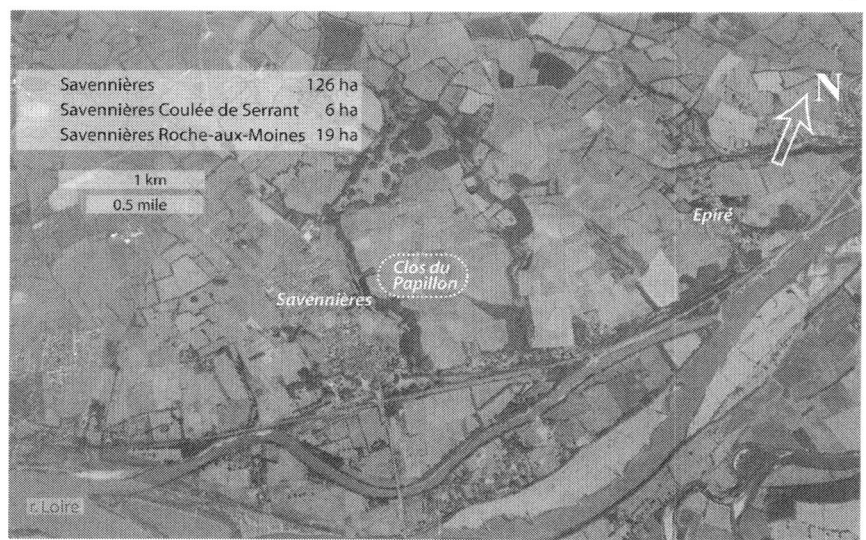

Savennières is a small appellation immediately north of the Loire. Coulée de Serrant and Roche-aux-Moines are separate appellations within it. Clos du Papillon is one of the most important vineyards.

"Life is a permanent fight against time," Nicolas said as he rushed in for our meeting at Château Roche aux Moines. The weather had suddenly turned sunny after three weeks of rain, and there was no wind, so he had been out in the vineyard organizing the workers to take advantage of the break in the weather to spray sulfur to protect the vines against fungal infections. "We can protect the vines for the next month by spraying now," he explains. "The sulfur we are spreading this morning comes from a mine. It is a natural product as opposed to coming from the petrochemical industry," he adds. Committed to the biodynamic approach, he has had a widespread influence on viticulture, as well as locally influencing style in Savennières.

"Often Savennières is too shallow; it would be improved by more maturity. My belief is that a bit of maturity is part of the taste. We harvest four times over three weeks, looking to get the grapes at each round at the same point of maturity. I don't look for late harvests, but I do wait for maturity," Nicolas says. This results in a powerful savory flavor spectrum, often accentuated by a touch of

The famous Coulée de Serrant is in the foreground; behind it is the Clos des Moines, with the Château de la Roche aux Moines at the far end of the vineyard. The Loire runs parallel on the left.

botrytis resulting from the late harvest; sometimes there is a little residual sugar.

Botrytis is desirable in sweet white wine (where it increases concentration and brings a delicious honeyed piquancy), it is ruinous in red wine (where the flavors clash), and in dry white wine... it is unusual. For most styles of white wine, especially those where freshness is the main criterion, botrytis is considered undesirable, but Savennières is one of the rare places where you find botrytis in dry wine. It tends to be confined to top sites, where late harvest is possible. As Charles Sydney, a broker in the Loire, comments, "Given Chenin's tendency to be acidic, it is essential to wait until the grape reaches full phenolic maturity before harvesting... A harvest with no rot is very unlikely to be ripe." The tendency seems to be to harvest early for freshness in entry-level wines, but to harvest later for more complexity in top wines. Other examples of dry wines relying on late harvest are Baumard's Trie Spéciale, a selection of more mature berries, sometimes but not necessarily botrytized, and Domaine du Closel's Clos du Papillon. In Savennières, botrytis is an

Reference Wines for dry white Anjou	
Savennières	Domaine Baumard, Clos du Papillon Domaine du Closel, Clos du Papillon Château d'Epiré, Cuvée Spéciale
Savennières Coulée de Serrant	Château Roche aux Moines
Savennières Roches-aux-Moines	Château Pierre Bise
Saumur	Domaine des Roches Neuves, L'Insolite
Anjou	Philippe Delesvaux, Cuvée Authentique Domaine Richou, Les Rogeries Domaine Eric Morgat, Litus
Vin de France	La Sansonnière, Les Fourchades

exception, but in Savennières Roches-aux-Moines, it is more common, since the eight producers seem to have a general policy of later harvest.

Nicolas Joly makes wine in all three appellations and the style of late harvest definitely trumps appellation differences, at least to the extent that the wines unmistakably come from a single producer. Yet Coulée de Serrant is more intense than the Savennières Roche-aux-Moins (Clos de la Bergerie), which is more intense than the Savennières (Le Vieux Clos). While this validates the appellation hierarchy, it bypasses the question of whether there is a difference in *character* or just an increased potential for achieving higher ripeness. Claude Papon at Château Pierre Bise also produces Savennières in a mature style, and his Roche-aux-Moines and Savennières Clos de Coulaine are variations on a theme, with Roche-aux-Moines fruitier, but Coulaine in fact more interestingly savory. The producer seems more important than the appellation in determining overall style.

The Whites of Saumur

For the most part, the whites of Saumur tend to be nondescript, but there's an exception at Brézé, a small area just to the south of Saumur, surrounded by the red wine appellation of Saumur-Champigny. The most famous dry white wine in Anjou used to come from here.

The wines of the Château de Brézé are reputed to have been common in the royal courts of Europe in the fifteenth century, to the point at which they later became known as Chenin de Brézé. An elevated site, sitting on a hill of tuffeau (local limestone), Brézé is dominated by the Château de Brézé, and when the AOC of Saumur-Champigny was established in 1957, its owner, Comte de Colbert, demanded that Brézé should have its own AOC because its terroir was so superior. Because of the poor quality of the wines-"an entire century of relatively terrible wines from one of the best sites in the Loire," is one description—the demand was refused, and M. le Comte then declined to be included in Saumur-Champigny. As a

Will the wines of Brezé be restored to their former glory as the best whites of Anjou?

result, the red wines as well as the whites are classified only as Saumur.

Today's best white wine from Brézé is no doubt Clos Rougeard's, with great purity of fruits showcasing the typical cereal/savory notes of Chenin Blanc, and a steely minerality that makes you think of Puligny Montrachet. The Château de Brézé itself is being renovated, and together with the efforts of other producers such as Domaine Guiberteau, we may see Brézé restored as a significant vineyard site.

Sweet Wines of Anjou

Facing Savennières on the south side of the Loire, the focus turns to sweet wines. When conditions are right, Chenin Blanc is a great grape for making sweet wine. Those herbal or even vegetal characteristics that producers have struggled to control in dry wines by obtaining greater ripeness provide the necessary counterpoise to lift the sweet wine above mere sweetness into complexity. And natural high acidity helps to keep the wine refreshing instead of cloying.

All the same, the style of the top wines can change dramatically from year to year, depending on the level of botrytis. From 2011 to 2013, there was little botrytis. When this happens the sweet wines are made by *passerillage*, effectively a desiccation of the grapes. This concentrates sugar, but does not give the delicious piquancy resulting from the growth of the botrytis fungus on the skin of the grapes.

The area of the Coteaux du Layon, where the best sweet wines are made, is defined by the river Layon, a tributary that runs into the Loire just to the west of Savennières. It has to be said that most Coteaux du Layon wines are rather ordinary, often only just above offdry sweetness, but the top areas, Quarts de Chaume, Bonnezeaux, and Chaume, are the glory of sweet wine in Anjou: in good years when levels of botrytis are high, they can rival Sauternes. But the reputation of the area has suffered from recent controversies, first about the descriptions of the appellations, and then about what techniques should be permitted.

Coteaux du Layon extends south of the Loire around the Layon river. The northern part of the area is the Coteaux du Layon Villages. The top three appellations are Quarts de Chaume, Chaume, and Bonnezaux.

Coteaux du Layon is the generic description for the entire area, but there is a higher level of Coteaux du Layon Villages, and six villages are allowed to append their name to the label. Chaume was; recognized as the best of them, but was somewhat overshadowed, by Quarts de Chaume, the best appellation for sweet wine in Anjou. When INAO decided in 2003 to promote Chaume to Chaume Premier Cru des Coteaux du Layon, there was a furious objection by the producers of Quarts de Chaume, who felt that the natural hierarchy was being revised. After a long argument, it was agreed in 2010 that Quarts de Chaume should be described as a grand cru, allowing Chaume to be described as premier cru. Curiously, Bonnezeaux, which is usually regarded as almost the equal of Quarts de Chaume, is not given grand or premier cru status (nor is Savennières, as there are no crus for dry white wines).

"Making great sweet wines in the Loire is risky," admits Gilles Bigot at Château de Fesles. This is true everywhere that sweet wine

Botrytis develops unevenly in the bunch. Some berries have only speckles of botrytis while others are completely desiccated. This requires berries to be picked individually in successive passes through the vineyard.

is made, of course, and the reputations of sweet wine appellations really depend on how reliably they develop botrytis. The advantage of the region is that mist rises from the Layon river in Autumn mornings, is trapped by the rolling hills on either side of the river, and then blows off in the afternoons. This allows botrytis to develop, but prevents it from turning to rot.

Quarts de Chaume is situated close to the Layon river; in fact it touches the river at some points. Its great reputation stems from the fact that it's the most susceptible area to botrytis. The hill of Chaume, which lies between the village of Chaume and the river, protects the vineyards from wind, helping to sustain more botrytis. Farther away from the river, Chaume does not usually achieve as much botrytis concentration.

For Quarts de Chaume Grand Cru, yields must be below 20 hl/ha and grapes can be harvested only if they have more than 298 g/l sugar, equivalent to potential alcohol of 18%. This means that grapes are required to have so much sugar that after fermentation comes to an end, at least 85 g/l residual sugar should remain, but in a good vintage there will be a lot more. Claude Papin, president of the Syndicat, says that, "The typicity of Quarts de Chaume should come from the terroir and climate of each vintage and not from

Mist rises over the Quarts de Chaume in the morning, but blows off in the af-
ternoon, creating ideal conditions for development of botrytis. Courtesy
Domaine Baumard.

wine-making techniques." This refers to the controversy as to whether techniques should be allowed to increase concentration during vinification.

The technique in question is called cryo-extraction. It mimics a feature of making ice wine, when berries are allowed to hang on the vine into the winter, until it becomes cold enough for them to freeze. They are harvested at night in the frozen state, and pressed immediately, while still frozen. Ice crystals that have formed within the berries effectively remove some of the water, which increases the concentration of the must. Large berries are more susceptible, because they have more water. Cryo-extraction creates a similar situation artificially by putting very mature berries into a freezer for a few hours before they are pressed.

Should cryo-extraction be used to make a wine such as Quarts de Chaume, I asked Florent Baumard, who has one of the largest holdings in the appellation, and is embroiled in controversy about his use of the technique. "First we should talk about cryo-selection not cryo-extraction, cryo-extraction is an improper term. We select grapes in the vineyard, but the berries are very delicate and easily ruined, when you try to remove individual berries (that you don't want) you can damage the others. [So we put] the berries into cold chambers for several hours below freezing temperature, and when you press, the juice comes from the more mature berries. This is a supplementary selection, not a concentration." Yet the question remains: is the wine as good when concentration is increased by cryo-extraction compared to botrytis or passerillage (desiccation) in the vineyard?

Florent's main objection is that people should not tell him how to make good wine. (Welcome to France!) "People say that cryo-selection abolishes the expression of terroir, but these wines—13 vintages of Quarts de Chaume—are all completely different. Contrary to views that it's not authentic, cryo-selection magnifies the terroir." It's a fair point that Baumard's Quarts de Chaume, irrespective of whether and to what extent cryo-extraction was used in any year, is one of the great wines of the appellation. But it's also a fair point that the technique bypasses the expectations of the consumer who is paying a hefty premium for Quarts de Chaume based on the fact that it's extremely expensive to select berries individually by successive passes through the vineyard.

Producers have agreed to ban the technique from the 2020 vintage. But it's surprising that while there is controversy about cryo-extraction, there's no general criticism of the fact that chaptalization is allowed in Coteaux du Layon (it is no longer permitted in Quarts de Chaume). For a dry wine, chaptalization changes the character indirectly, because all the added sugar is converted to alcohol. For a sweet wine, however, chaptalization must mean that

Reference Wines for sweet Anjou	
Coteaux du Layon	Domaine Philippe Delesvaux
Coteaux du Layon Villages	Domaine Vincent Ogereau, Harmonie
Coteaux du Layon Chaume	Château Soucherie
Quarts de Chaume	Domaine Baumard Château Pierre Bise
Bonnezeaux	Château de Fesles

the added sugar ends up directly sweetening the wine. The effect is just the same as adding sugar to the completed wine (which would be illegal). The better producers don't use chaptalization, of course, but the reputation of the appellation is undermined by the practice, and it's hard to see how any sweet wine appellation can have credibility when chaptalization is allowed.

Touraine

Moving from Anjou to Touraine, the balance shifts to red wines. The best come from Cabernet Franc at the western edge of Touraine, essentially parallel to the reds from the eastern edge of Anjou. Aside from Cabernet Franc, the other significant black varieties are Grolleau and Gamay, both light and fruity, and used mostly

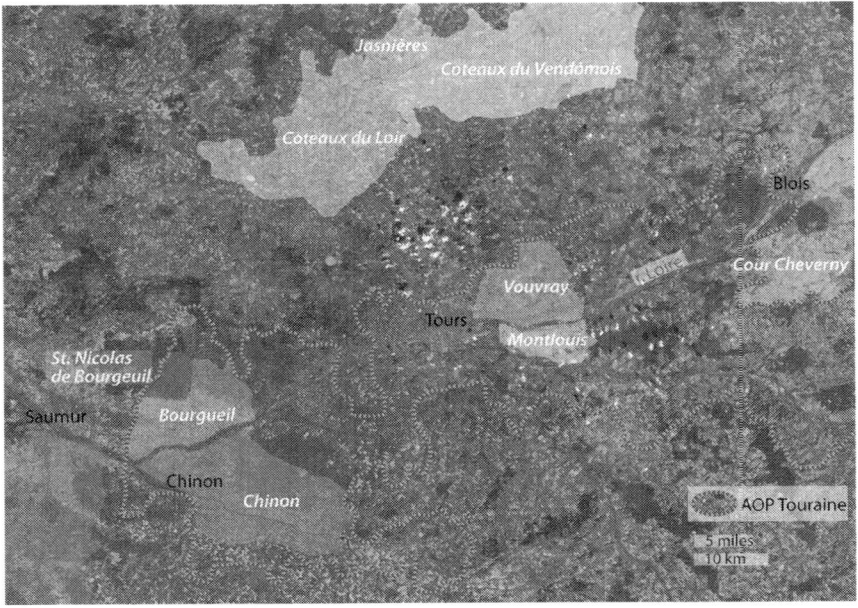

The vineyards of Touraine stretch from Chinon to Blois. The regions adjacent to Anjou at the western edge focus on reds; the rest of the region focuses on whites. The generic AOP Touraine includes geographical subdivisions of Touraine-Azay-le-Rideau, Touraine-Amboise, and Touraine-Mesland. Other appellations lie to the north.

Are these the oldest vines in France? This plot of Romorantin was planted around 1850.

for a softening effect in blending, as well as comprising a major part of rosés in both Anjou and Touraine.

Gamay is vinified as a single variety in the Touraine Gamay, but it is rarely a match even for Beaujolais. An exception comes from the eastern edge of Touraine, where Henry Marionnet at Domaine de la Charmoise makes monovarietal Gamays from both conventional plantings (vines on rootstocks) and from *franc de pied*, vines planted on their own roots. In fact, several varieties have been planted on their own roots, offering a rare chance to compare wines from grafted versus ungrafted vines.

The impetus for this experiment was the discovery of a small plot of very old vines of the variety Romorantin (which is the basis for the Cour-Cheverny appellation). These vines appear to have been planted well before phylloxera, and are a candidate for the oldest vines in France. They are still thriving and make a magnificent wine.

Away from the western border, the rest of Touraine is generally devoted to white wines, ranging from dry to sweet. The heart of production for quality white wine is the single appellation of Vouvray, north of the Loire just to the east of Tours, together with Montlouis across the river to the south. Because Vouvray is at the limit between Atlantic and Continental influences, where winds from the sea and winds from inland meet, vintage has a particularly strong effect.

Styles of Vouvray

There's huge variation in Vouvray as to whether still wine is made (in the better vintages) or whether it's converted into a sparkling wine (in less successful years). The choice of style may not be made until September. With the recent warming trend, sparkling wine production has decreased, and the proportion of sweet and semi-sweet among the still wines has increased.

A generation ago a minority of harvests gave sweet wines; now it is a majority. Harvesting has moved two weeks earlier since 2000, and botrytis occurs more often, especially when there is an Indian summer into October. Now the problem can be lack of acidity whereas previously it was lack of alcohol.

The wide range of styles with regards to sweetness makes it difficult to define typical character for Vouvray. Producers mostly do not specialize: wine styles are determined more by vintage conditions than by choice. A tasting at even a small producer is a protracted affair, because all producers make wines at all sweetness levels: there's usually sec (dry) and demi-sec (off-dry), and when conditions permit, moelleux (sweet) and liquoreux (very sweet). "We are just at a point of balance here, one talks of the Loire as the northern limit for grape growing. So there can be great differences depending on vintage. This is why Vouvray varies so much—that it is the one appellation of France where all styles of wine are possible," says François Pinon. This has its advantages, however; when I asked François if he had a problem with alcohol levels being pushed up by global warming, the answer was simple. "Not at all, if that happens I make a demi-sec." His general view is that, "Chenin is not an aromatic variety, it is very versatile, a chameleon, and its character depends on the terroir and vintage. In 2011 we made

Tufa rock, a yellow limestone, is common in Anjou and Touraine, usually covered only by shallow soil.

mostly Pétillant, in 2003 mostly moelleux. Our philosophy is to get the best berries possible, but Nature decides..."

Personally, I am inclined to find the most interest in the wines at both ends of the spectrum. The dry wines can show Chenin Blanc character, although it can be partly obscured by the tendency to leave just a little residual sugar (wines can be labeled dry even if they have more than the usual limit of 4 g/l residual sugar under an exception that applies when acidity is high enough). When you quiz producers or sommeliers in the region as to whether a wine is dry, the usual euphemism is to say, "Well, it's fruity."

Versatile but unpredictable might be a fair summary of style in Vouvray. "How dry is the sec?" I asked Anthony Hwang, the new proprietor at Domaine Huët. "It depends from year to year. If acidity is high, fermentation is stopped sooner; the objective is to taste dry." At the other extreme, where wines have sweetness at the high end of the moelleux range or into liquoreux, intense concentration can also bring out Chenin Blanc typicity in the style of dessert wine: sweet, honeyed (if there has been botrytis), nutty, often with strong acidity.

The producers of Vouvray mostly don't seem to believe in truly dry wines: the informal retention of the sec-tendre category may indicate where their heart lies. This has more sugar than qualifies for sec, but not enough to be demi-sec (what the Germans would call halbtrocken or half-dry). However, it is not legal to use sec-tendre on the label. My main complaint about the intermediate levels of sugar is that when the wines are young, the sweetness tends to obscure the character of the grape and give a somewhat one dimensional impression. For me the line is crossed into losing typicity around the transition to demi-sec.

With that tendency towards residual sugar—even in the nominally dry wines—you might think Vouvray would be the perfect white wine for the Coca Cola generation. There seems to be an attitude here (somewhat akin to the old attitude in Germany before the trocken trend swept through Riesling) that a little sugar is needed to bring out flavor and to counteract intrinsic bitterness in Chenin Blanc. My main concern about Vouvray is that there isn't always enough flavor concentration to stand up to the sugar (until you get to the very sweet). As the sweetness category is often not indicated on the label for wines that are sec or demi-sec, the only safe attitude is to assume a Vouvray is likely to be off-dry unless there is specific information to the contrary.

Character for me shows most clearly in the sec and moelleux categories, but you do have to taste them at the right point in development to see this most clearly. "You see the purity of the terroir straight away with the dry wines, but you have to wait to see it with sweet wines," Anthony Hwang believes. "Chenin Blanc takes at least five years to show its typicity. The more concentration of sugar you have, the longer you have to wait. A sec will show after 3 years, a demi-sec after 5 years, a moelleux after 5-10 years, and the very sweet wines only after ten years. The sugar hides the expression of the variety," says Bernard Fouquet of Domaine des Aubuisières.

Vouvray runs for 20 kilometers along the north bank of the Loire. The best vineyards are the premier coteaux, immediately beyond the alluvial soil along the river, and around the town of Vouvray, but the appellation extends well inland. The soil type is

The top vineyards of Vouvray are on the slopes just above the town, overlooking the church.

known locally as perruches, a greenish clay containing large flinty pebbles. This is considered to give the most delicate, even austere, wines. Beyond, on the plateau, the soils have more clay over the typical tufa rock, a soft yellow limestone, that is characteristic of the area, but there is significant heterogeneity.

The character of Vouvray, or perhaps one should say the characters of Vouvray, are captured by Domaine Huët, one of the oldest, and certainly the most famous, producer. The domain holds three of Vouvray's most important vineyards and makes wines at all levels of sweetness from each of them. So here is an opportunity to compare the effects of terroir and sweetness. Le Haut Lieu is one of the highest points on the plateau just above the town, facing south towards the town. It has heavy clay soil over the tufa rock. Just below, Le Mont has the classic perruches soil. Overlooking the church in Vouvray, and dating from the eighth century, Clos du Bourg is the oldest vineyard in the appellation. This has the shallowest soil, only a meter deep, directly above the tufa rock.

The reputation of the domain was made with its sweet wines, especially at the moelleux level, but the dry wines offer a striking demonstration of the effect of terroir on Chenin Blanc: character goes from forward and supple at Le Haut Lieu, to broad and rich at Le Bourg, and tight and backward at Le Mont (always the last vineyard to be picked).

Across the river, the terroir is more homogeneous in Montlouis. The appellation forms a small triangle lying between the Loire and Cher rivers. Although there are some soils of perruches, they contain less schist than in Vouvray, making the wines of Montlouis softer. Montlouis makes the same range of wines as Vouvray, from sec to moelleux. With vineyards running down to the river in Montlouis, you might expect more focus on botrytis, but the problem here is that it's not usually hot enough; so if there is rot it is not necessarily noble, and botrytized wine is less common than in Vouvray. Whenever it is possible to compare Vouvray and Montlouis directly from the same producer, the difference shows most clearly in the moelleux wines, where Vouvray has more intensity than the Montlouis.

Even with the increase in the proportion of still wines resulting from warmer vintages, more than half of Vouvray's production remains in sparkling wine. Production today includes two styles: Crémant (Méthode Champenoise) and Pétillant, which has lower pressure. However, because most producers make sweet wine *faute de mieux*, it's hard to find examples of real quality.

Jasnières

The northernmost vineyards in the west of France are about 50 kilometers north of the city of Tours, centered on the Loir river (with no "e" at the end, this runs parallel with the Loire). The terroir has the usual base of tufa, but it's cooler here than in the appellations in the center of Touraine. This is an area that was devoted to Pineau d'Aunis from around the ninth century, and the Coteaux du Loir is effectively the last remaining place where it is still grown in France. In better vintages it makes a red wine, but in poorer vintages may be used for rosé.

The best of the three northern appellations is Jasnières, where there are some fine, almost delicate, white wines from Chenin Blanc. Most are dry or demi-sec, but there are moelleux wines in good vintages. Comparing the relationship to the most famous vine-

Reference Wines for white Touraine	
Vouvray (sec)	François Pinon
Vouvray (demi-sec)	Vincent Carême, Tendre
Vouvray (moelleux)	Domaine Huët, Clos du Bourg
Vouvray (liquoreux)	Domaine Huët, Cuvée Constance
Montlouis (sec)	François Chidaine, Les Bournais
Jasnières (sec)	Domaine Bellivière, Calligramme
Chinon	Bernard Baudry, La Croix Boisée Charles Joguet, Clos de la Plante Martin

yards of Germany, Jacqueline Friedrich says, "If Rheingau is Savennières then Jasnières is Mosel".

There is some Chardonnay in Touraine, as AOP Touraine allows Chardonnay to be used but not to be stated on the label, although monovarietal Sauvignon Blanc can be named on the label. An unnamed Touraine AOP Blanc may therefore be Chardonnay rather than Sauvignon, although strictly speaking the proportion of Chardonnay is supposed to be limited to 20%. There is in fact some monovarietal Chardonnay, but when it is presented for approval, the producer describes it as a blend, another example of the tricks producers are forced to play to survive in the system.

Cabernet Franc

Widely planted in Anjou and Touraine, Cabernet Franc is the most important black grape of the Loire. A major part of it goes to make Cabernet d'Anjou, which although named for the variety, is in fact a rosé, not a red wine. Both the rosé and the red can also include Cabernet Sauvignon, although this is not common.

The appellations for red wine are adjacent at the border between Anjou and Touraine. Saumur-Champigny has the greatest reputation in Anjou. Immediately across the river in Touraine, Bour-

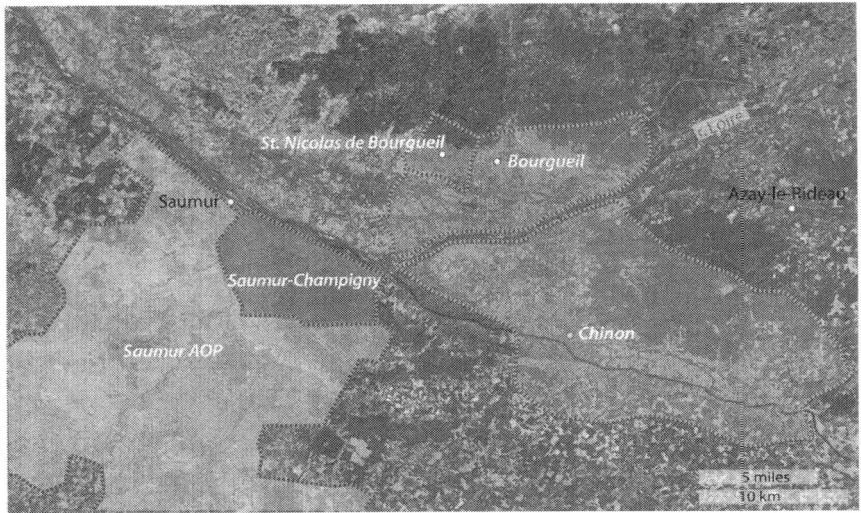

The top regions for Cabernet Franc lie at the border between Anjou and Touraine, with Saumur and Saumur-Champigny of Anjou adjacent to St. Nicolas de Bourgueil, Bourgueil, and Chinon of Touraine.

guil is better known than St. Nicolas de Bourgueil, but Chinon is much the largest red wine appellation. The burning question is whether each appellation has a distinct character.

"The difference with the other (red wine) appellations is that Chinon has more diversity. Typicity really depends on the soils," says winemaker Kevin Fontaine at Domaine Charles Joguet in Chinon. "There are really two styles: the fruity ones where the fruit overpowers the wine; and the others that are more vins de garde where the tannins are more evident and drive the structure." At Château Hureau, Philippe Vatan agrees. "Chinon is larger so there is greater variety of terroirs. The character of Saumur-Champigny is that the tannins are sterner. But there is more resemblance between Saumur-Champigny and Chinon made in the same style than among the wines of either individual appellation."

Chinon is divided into roughly three parts: the plain, the coteaux (slopes), and the plateau. Along the river Vienne towards the southern border, only some of the plain, where the terroir is generally sandy, is considered appropriate for AOP wine. Extending up the slopes of the coteaux going north, the best terroirs are often cal-

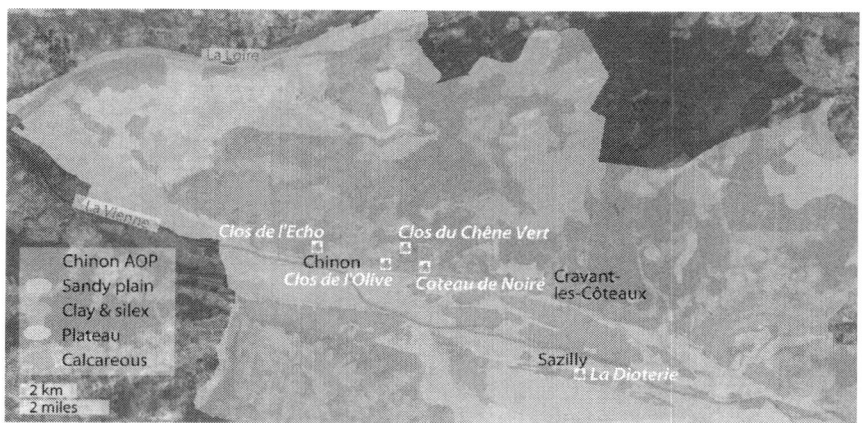

The Chinon AOP extends from its northern boundary at the Loire to south of the river Vienne. Most of the top vineyards lie in a line between Chinon and Cravant-les-Côteaux.

careous, forming a line more or less parallel with the river Vienne to its north. This is where most of the famous single-vineyard Cabernet Francs originate. Then up above lies the plateau, where the soils are sand and silt, based on subsoils of sand and clay with some flint.

While there may be some stereotypes for the appellations, in reality each appellation offers a range of styles. The general tendency is to lighten up the wines, and at entry level the wines tend to follow a similar style: Cabernet Franc is not a variety to make overtly fruity wine, but relatively speaking, the wines are light, fruity, fresh, and approachable for drinking in the short term. But top producers are increasingly focusing on demonstrating the effects of terroir. Sometimes this is achieved by cuvées from single vineyards with different terroirs, sometimes by assemblage from several small plots all with the same sort of terroir. The old idea of assemblage from lots that come from plots with different, complementary, properties is no longer fashionable.

Some producers make a range of wines from entry level up to top cuvées. The difficulty here is distinguishing between them, as there is no system to indicate the underlying character of the terroir. In Burgundy, you know at once that a Bourgogne will be a producer's simplest wine, and a very different affair from a premier or grand cru. In the appellations of Anjou and Touraine, there is noth-

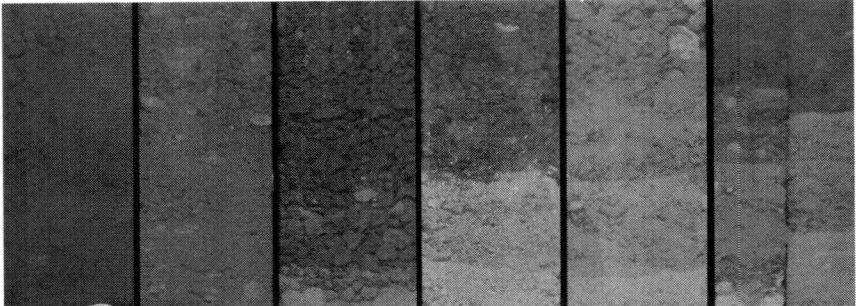

Chinon has a variety of terroirs. From left to right these soil samples show: alluvial soil near the river; gravel from the plain; clay and yellow limestone from the slopes; clay and white limestone; highly calcareous soils; sand and limestone from the plateau (two examples). Courtesy Domaine Bernard Baudry.

ing to distinguish the cuvées except the producer's individual names. Sometimes these may represent a generic wine, sometimes an assemblage from plots, sometimes a single vineyard. But seeing a wine in isolation—for example on a restaurant list where there is no external guide to quality—it can be impossible to place in the hierarchy.

There's almost as much Cabernet Franc in the Loire as in Bordeaux, but the difference is that in Bordeaux it is almost always part of a blend, whereas in the Loire it is most often vinified as a monovarietal. So it's really these Loire reds that offer the best opportunity to see the varietal character of Cabernet Franc. But different producers have very different ideas on how this should be achieved.

"There is an attitude in France that to make a grand vin you need to mature in barriques," said Jacques Couly, of Couly-Dutheil, the most famous producer of Cabernet Franc in Chinon. "But it's stupid to judge one wine by another. We shouldn't imitate what is happening elsewhere. The Loire doesn't really have a tradition of barriques; people have used all sorts of wood and other containers in the past. We should ask, is wood the right route? The idea is to put the fruit of Cabernet Franc first; we are the sole region in France to make wine solely from Cabernet Franc, why mask the flavors with wood? Everything now goes into stainless steel. This complicates things and means there must be more work in the vineyards because steel is pitiless in revealing the true character of the wine. It requires the Cabernet Franc to be completely mature." The immedi-

Clos de l'Echo is the only vineyard in the town of Chinon, and runs down from a plateau to the castle.

ate question is whether the wines have the same aging potential. Judged by the two most famous wines, Clos de l'Olive and Clos de l'Echo, there is increased purity of fruits without any loss of complexity.

The other great producer of Cabernet Franc in Chinon, Charles Joguet, pursues a traditional Burgundian policy of increasing oak exposure with the quality of the terroir. In fact, it was Charles Joguet who first introduced the idea of making cuvées from different terroirs when he came back to Sazilly from art studies in Paris in 1959. At that time, most Chinon was sold in bulk. "People thought he was crazy, he was an artist with odd ideas," says Anne-Charlotte Genet, whose family came into the winery in 1995 when Charles decided he wanted to return to art. The entry level cuvée is matured in cuve, but the top Clos du Chêne Vert spends 12-15 months in barriques of one to three years' age. Here there's a clear increase in complexity going up the hierarchy, with that elegant purity of Cabernet Franc most evident in the top cuvées. Coming from a variety of terroirs, the Joguet wines demonstrate the increase in complexity and weight with the progression from sand to gravel to limestone.

Cabernet Franc can certainly make vins de garde in the Loire, nowhere better demonstrated than by Yannick Amirault, who has vineyards in both Bourgueil and St. Nicolas de Bourgueil. "There's large diversity in terroir and no single typicity for either appellation. You can find the same types of soil in St. Nicolas or Bourgueil. St. Nicolas has a reputation for lighter wines but that's due to yields and the policies of the individual vignerons. In a blind tasting you cannot tell the difference between St. Nicolas, Bourgueil, and Chinon," he says. Once again there is a palpable increase in weight going from sand to limestone; all the wines here are relatively stern, but these are the most Cabernet Franc-ish wines in the appellations. Always vinified in wood, these wines bring out the more reserved side of Cabernet Franc.

Saumur-Champigny has the greatest reputation for Cabernet Franc in the Loire, and I am far from alone in regarding Clos Rougeard as its top producer, indeed as the greatest producer of red wine in the Loire. The wines are made by brothers Nady and Charlie Foucault (by Nady alone after Charlie died in 2015), who are famous for their reserve, but the three red cuvées of the domain absolutely shine out. Their U.S. importer, Joe Dressner, quotes Charles Joguet as saying: "There are two suns. One shines outside for everybody. The second shines in the Foucaults' cellar." Actually, the cellar consists of a rabbit warren of very cold, old caves carved out of the rock under the house. Intensity of Cabernet Franc increases through the three cuvées, the domain wine, Le Poyeux, and Le Bourg (from a single hectare behind the house on the main street in Chacé).

The major characteristic of the house style is the sheer purity of fruits. There is a wonderfully seamless, smooth edge to the Cabernet Franc; you feel you are tasting the unalloyed purity of the variety. Precisely delineated fruits are supported by a very fine underlying granular texture, with a surface sheen and hints of stone and tobacco. The reds are by far the best known, but the white (Le Brézé) is also very fine: concentrated, mineral, and savory.

There are other fine red wines in Saumur-Champigny and Chinon, but it is fair to say that nothing else I tasted on a recent visit to the region left me with that impression of seamless purity. I asked the Foucaults what is responsible for the difference at Clos Rougeard. "We had a chance, our parents never used herbicide; they were the only people in the appellation not to do so in the 1960s and 1970s. The other vignerons mocked us because we had weeds among the vines. And in the 1980s we were the only ones to mature our harvest in barriques; most people only used cuves," says Nady Foucault. The difference is so marked, it's hard to believe that is all there is to it! When pushed, all Nady would add was that they have kept the winemaking practices of their parents and grandparents. But with all due respect, I would be astonished if the wines were this fine two generations ago.

The Foucaults are conscious of the fact that their wines are different. "For thirty years we have been the only ones to respect the lieu-dits and to distinguish our wines by the Burgundian philosophy of climats... This was lost after the second world war when mechanization resulted in the destruction of the walls. Just as Beaujolais abandoned its climats with Beaujolais Nouveau, so Saumur-Champigny became a light, fresh, fruity wine... However, there's a tradition of vins de garde coming from the extraordinary diversity of terroir in Saumur and Saumur-Champigny, and at Chinon and Bourgueil also. Our grandparents distinguished their lieu-dits, and we have done the same, even if today INAO recommends against it... Bourg has always had a famous ability to age, and it would be scandalous to make a light wine to drink immediately," is Nady's general philosophy.

With some rare exceptions, such as Clos Rougeard, I do not think the red wines of Anjou benefit from long aging. Certainly the better wines of Saumur-Champigny, Bourgueil, and Chinon need at least a couple of years after release for the tannins to soften and for the fruits to show: to drink them upon release may be to miss their complexity. But although producers will say, "They can age for ten or fifteen years, no problem," I suspect most are at their best around five to six years after release, and any increasing development with

Reference Wines for Loire Cabernet Franc	
Saumur-Champigny	Clos Rougeard, Les Poyeux
Bourgueil	Catherine & Pierre Breton, Franc de Pied
St. Nicolas de Bourgueil	Yannick Amirault, Les Malgagnes
Chinon	Couly-Dutheil, Clos de l'Echo Charles Joguet, Clos du Chêne Vert

age may be offset by a decline in a fruit density. I would be inclined to drink the top wines between five and ten years after the vintage.

The Loire is pretty far north to grow Cabernet Franc. Even in Bordeaux, father south, ripening is not assured every year, and it's often a problem in the Loire (except perhaps for the Foucaults!) This raises the question: why not blend with another, softer, earlier-ripening variety, as they do, for example with Merlot in St. Emilion? In terms of varieties historically grown in the Loire, no other quality black variety is available; and of course the possibilities have now been set in stone by AOP rules. But in any case, although to do so might make a more reliable wine in most years, you would not get to see that wonderful purity of Cabernet Franc in the top years.

Sancerre

"Our white is one of the great wines of the world, with purity, finesse, and fruit. We have excellent terroir for Sauvignon Blanc. We have to keep our heads straight, not to be influenced by other regions of the world, and to keep the typicity that made our wines successful." That's the view from Catherine Corbeau-Mellot at Joseph Mellot in Sancerre. "Purity, finesse, and fruit" is a fair enough way to describe the best wines of Sancerre today; certainly this is a long way from the wines of twenty or thirty years ago that were often quite herbaceous and punishingly acid.

"Cat's pee" was the most common description for Sauvignon Blanc at this period. This was the consequence of failing to get the grapes ripe, but since then the view of Sauvignon Blanc has bifurcated. Its fame as a variety in New Zealand comes from pushing expression of Sauvignon's sharp, grassy tang: offset by ripe citrus fruits, this makes an attractive wine with bright, not to say aggressive, contrasts. Sancerre has taken another route, producing a more restrained wine, where the fruit spectrum tends to citrus, sometimes with grassy overtones, sometimes melding into stone fruits of peaches and apricots (but rarely into exotic fruits, such as the passion fruit often found in New Zealand). When I asked winemakers in Sancerre if they had been influenced by New Zealand's success with the variety, all denied any direct effect, but agreed that the modern consumer wants to see more fruit. Their view of the appro-

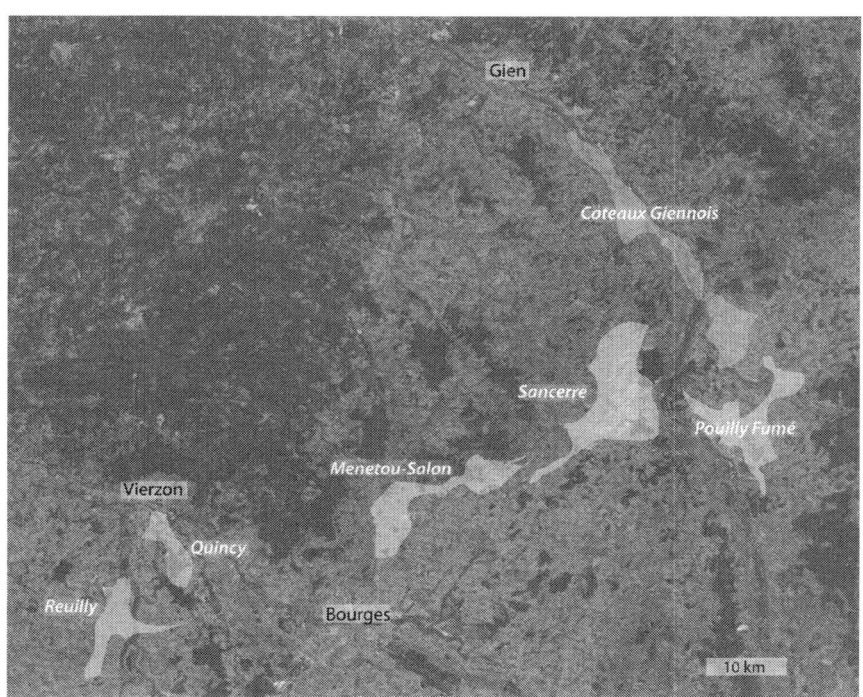

The major appellations of Loire Centre extend over 100 km on an east-west axis.

priate fruit, you might say, is more traditional than it is in New Zealand.

Loire Centre is the smallest part of the Loire in terms of vineyard area, and its individual appellations are relatively well separated. The vast majority of production in the region is monovarietal Sauvignon Blanc. In fact, Sancerre and Pouilly Fumé dominated the world supply of Sauvignon Blanc until New Zealand's rise to fame. By far the best known appellation in Loire Centre, Sancerre is the largest, extending over six communes, while Pouilly Fumé has about half the vineyard area on the other side of the river. The tiny area of Menetou-Salon is just to the west of Sancerre; Quincy and Reuilly are farther west. Sancerre has the most dramatic terrain, with really steep hills, whereas the vineyards between Reuilly and Menetou-Salon lie on rolling hills.

In the early nineteenth century, Sancerre produced mostly red wine. But Sauvignon Blanc has been planted in the area since the sixteenth century, and was used for producing white wine together with Pinot Gris and Chasselas. Sauvignon Blanc fell out of favor and was replaced by Chasselas (an over-productive, characterless variety), and then came back again after the phylloxera epidemic. But the reputation of the region for quality white wine is more recent. Before Appellation Contrôlée regulations put a stop to such shenanigans in 1936, much of the white wine was sent to Champagne to augment the local product; when this stopped, the Sancerre vineyards declined, until by 1960 there were only 600 ha. Today plantings are up to about 2,500 ha, with 80% of the production being dry white wine from Sauvignon Blanc.

The Centre is actually at the eastern edge of the Loire, but its name reflects the fact that it is central with regards to other vineyards in France. It is at a dividing point. (In terms of political units, Sancerre is part of the Loire while Pouilly-sur-Loire will appear on your GPS under Burgundy. In fact, Sancerre was more or less the western edge of the old Duchy of Burgundy in the Middle Ages.) To the west, the vineyards of Touraine are the Centre's immediate neighbor. Only a little farther in the other direction, to the east, are the vineyards of Burgundy. Chablis and Champagne are to the northeast: Paris is more or less directly north. The Loire Centre's geographical allegiance is connected more with Burgundy and Champagne to its east than with the rest of the Loire to the west; in fact, the same soil type runs from Loire Centre through Chablis to Champagne.

The Kimmeridgian Chain

This is Kimmeridgian marl, a limestone with clay formed by marine deposits many millions of years ago. (Occasionally large marine fossils turn up in the vineyards.) The wine-producing areas are geological islands in what geologist James Wilson called the Kimmeridgian Chain. It's most famous in Chablis, but similar terroir is found in Sancerre, and to a lesser extent in the other appellations of Loire Centre. Champagne, of course, is also famous for its chalk deposits, and the northern end of the Kimmeridgian chain extends into the vineyards of the Aube, a southern outpost of the Champagne region. It's remarkable that these three parts of the

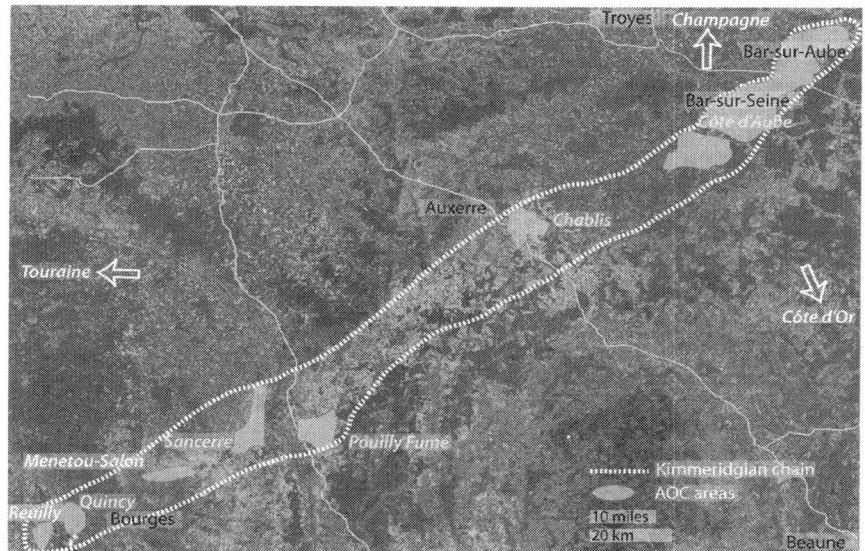

A band of Kimmeridgian terroir runs for 150 miles from the most eastern vineyards of the Loire, through Chablis, to the vineyards of the Aube.

Kimmeridgian chain produce such different wines: Sauvignon Blanc, Chablis, and Champagne.

If appellations were defined by geology, the Kimmeridgian Chain would be a single appellation (although it would show some climatic differences from one end to the other). The similarities along the Kimmeridgian chain are emphasized by the wines of St. Bris, a small area near Chablis that is Burgundy's outpost for producing Sauvignon Blanc. Its relationship to Sancerre makes you realize that the focus on Chardonnay in one place and on Sauvignon Blanc in the other is as much due to historical accident as geological imperatives.

Sancerre is the most complex of the appellations of the Centre geologically, but the same principal three kinds of terroir are found throughout the region. The Kimmeridgian soils are called Terres Blanches locally, describing their white appearance. They are common in Pouilly Fumé, prominent in Sancerre, and peter out in Quincy and Reuilly. Caillottes describes the small pebbles that cover the lower slopes of hills, and which consist of Portlandian or Oxfordian limestone (a bit harder in structure). Silex is a completely different type, essentially flint with varying amounts of clay.

The calcareous soils of Sancerre appear white in winter.

A major fault running through Sancerre is the dividing line between terroirs. Most of the limestone is to the west of the fault; most of the flint is to the east, where it's a strong influence in Pouilly Fumé, but it's not a hard and fast rule. The big question is what difference this makes to the style of the wine, and whether there is a consistent typicity for each appellation.

Sancerre versus Pouilly Fumé

"The Central Loire train's engine is Sancerre. The coaches are, by order of recognition, Pouilly, Menetou-Salon, Quincy and Reuilly," says Claude Lafond of Reuilly. Although Pouilly Fumé may be almost as well as known as Sancerre, it's fair to say that the others are less well established. Until recently it was difficult to make direct comparisons, because producers were entirely local, but now there's something of a move for producers to make wines from more than one appellation. "Menetou-Salon is being bought up by foreigners from Sancerre," one producer goes so far as to say.

Where it's possible to make comparisons, Reuilly, Quincy, and Menetou-Salon tend to be lighter weight; I would not say the fruits

The three major terroirs are Terres Blanches (Kimmeridgian limestone with some clay), Caillottes (small pebbles of Portlandian limestone), and Silex (small pebbles of flint). Terre Blanches is most common around Chavignol, Caillottes around Bué, and Silex to the east of Sancerre and in Pouilly Fumé, but all three terroirs are found in all areas.

are necessarily less ripe, but they seem less intense. The terrain at Reuilly is sandier and less calcareous, giving white wines with more freshness and less intensity; Menetou-Salon has more heterogeneity (including a rare patch of silex), and Paul-Henry Pellé sees the wines as elegant but not as "large" as Sancerre. The reds also tend to be a little tighter than those of Sancerre, but much depends on conditions of cultivation. "We're right at the limit of ripeness," says Paul-Henry.

When you ask producers what difference they see between Sancerre and Pouilly Fumé, there is usually agreement that there's a difference, but little consensus as to how to describe it. Freshness and minerality are the qualities always mentioned for both appellations. Personally, I've usually found Pouilly Fumé to be a little rounder, a little less aggressive. This may be because of the higher proportion of flint in its vineyards. "It keeps warm during the day, and at night it can be two or three degrees warmer than limestone, so the berries reach ripeness sooner. And drainage is better," says Frédéric Jacquet at Joseph Mellot. But if this is historically true, the difference has been narrowed by the move to greater ripeness. In any case, today's focus on expressing individual terroirs means that the difference between limestone and flint may be more important than the difference between Sancerre and Pouilly Fumé.

Is there any single typicity for Sancerre? "Only that it is Sauvignon," says Stéphane Riffault at Domaine Claude Riffaut. "Each vig-

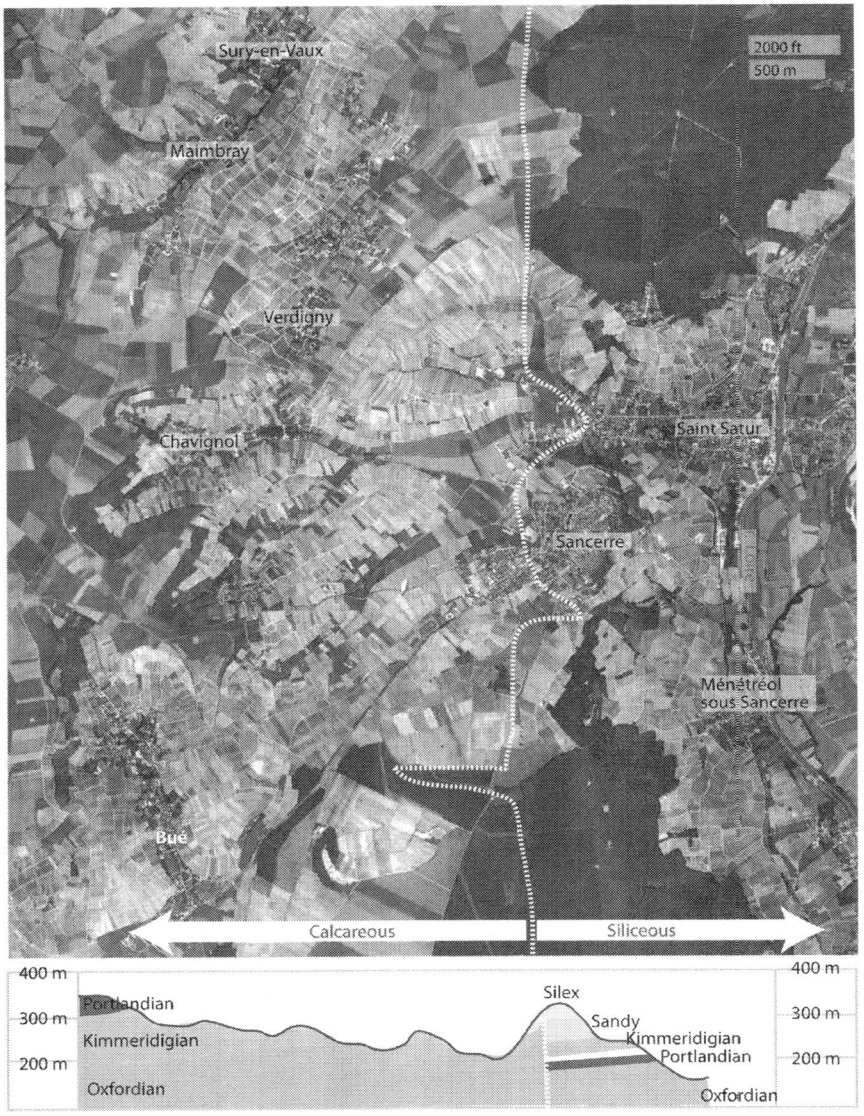

Sancerre vineyards are mostly to the west of the geological fault (dotted white line) that separates calcareous soils from the siliceous soils on the eastern side (map at top). A cross section through a line running from Chavignol to Sancerre (bottom) shows that Portlandian soils are found on the hilltops, Kimmeridgian soils on the slopes, and Oxfordian soils at the bottom. The structure is different to the east of the fault line. The villages of Sancerre AOP are Sury-en-Vaux, Maimbray, Verdigny, Chavignol, Bué, and Sancerre.

neron has his own manner of working and his own typicity." Variation is enhanced by the move towards making wines from single vineyards, which represents a real change in attitude. Sancerre used to be made by assemblage from different terroirs. Many producers still make an entry level cuvée based on assemblage; this is pretty much a necessity for any significant volume of production. But now the best vineyards are often singled out for individual cuvées, supplemented by cuvées that merge lots from parcels sharing similar terroir. The idea that a cuvée should represent a specific terroir is a real reversal from the old objective of gaining complexity by blending between different areas.

Sancerre made an early decision to focus on the single name of the appellation, so the six individual villages within the AOP are not allowed to attach their names to the label. Yet producers think of their wines in terms of the villages; and wine lists at local restaurants, for example, usually divide the wines according to village. The names of individual sites are a guide to quality and style. The top vineyards are located in Chavignol and Bué. In Chavignol, the best is Les Monts Damnés, followed by La Grande Côte and Le Cul de Beaujeu. In Bué, the best is Le Chêne Marchand—"Whenever a

The hilltop town of Sancerre dominates the local vineyards.

Mont Damnés, one of the most famous vineyards of Sancerre, rises up steeply immediately behind the village of Chavignol.

winemaker has Chêne Marchand, it is always the most complex wine in his cellar," says Clément Pinard—followed by Grande (and Petite) Chemarin. Bué's soils have more compact chalk, and less marl and clay, than Chavignol, so tend to finesse and precision, sometimes almost perfumed, whereas Chavignol tends to more powerful expression. There's general consensus on which vineyards are superior, but a tacit agreement that it would be too divisive to try to achieve any formal classification of Crus. "The difficulties and arguments about classification in St. Emilion are a warning about trying to make a classification," says Gilles Crochet of Domaine Lucien Crochet.

The Character of Sauvignon Blanc

Chavignol is famous for its goat cheese, the Crottin de Chavignol, which is supposed to be a perfect match for the wine. However, the locals chuckle when you ask, where are the goats? On the tops of the hills, they say at first. When you point out that the hills are now covered with vineyards right up to the summits,

Goats were still being kept at Chavignol in the 1970s, but now have been completely displaced by vineyards. (The AOC of Crottin de Chavignol was created in 1976, just before the goats began to disappear. Now they are mostly in Cosne-sur-Loire, a few miles to the north. The cuverie of Henri Bourgeois now stands where the goats used to roam.)

they admit there are no longer any goats in Chavignol: the vineyards proved sufficiently profitable that the goats were completely displaced during the eighties. The goats are now in Cosne-sur-Loire, a few miles away, but the AOP remains Crottin de Chavignol. But does it still make a perfect match with Sancerre? The pairing was based on a period when the wine was grassy and herbaceous, with its punishing acidity a match for the sharp tang of the cheese. Is the desertion of the goats a metaphor for the change in style of Sancerre, which with sweet citrus and stone fruits is perhaps no longer any more a match for the cheese than the goats are for the town.

The change in the view of varietal typicity has come with the move to picking later. "In the seventies, people harvested early, they were scared of rain and rot, now with globalization we are obliged to harvest at greater maturity. But it should not go too far, it would be ridiculous if all the wines tasted of mango," says Gilles Crochet. The time of harvest is really critical. "The window of harvest for Sauvignon Blanc is just four days for each block: you have to be in that time if you want to display varietal character," says Jean-Laurent Vacheron. Typicity disappears at over-ripeness in the same way that it's harder to see at under-ripeness.

Emphasis on terroir is common now. Yet producer style, especially the decision on time of harvest, has an equally large effect, creating an almost-Burgundian situation in which each producer expresses differences between terroirs in terms of his own style. This may take the form, for example, of a shift in the balance between citrus (emphasized by less ripe sites) and stone fruits (showing up as fruit becomes riper). Alphonse Mellot (père) explains the effect: "The change in flavor comes from the increased fruit maturity. When Sancerre becomes really ripe it loses more tartaric acid than malic acid, and it's the tartaric that gives the citrus impression."

The appellations of the Loire Centre now offer a complete gamut of Sauvignon Blanc flavors. Herbaceousness and cat's pee are rare, but wines in the traditional mode may still show grassy aromas and sweaty overtones. In the mid range, fruits become sweet citrus, ranging from lemon and grapefruit to a delicious touch of lime. Stone fruits begin to creep in for the producers who pick later, with apricots and peaches adding to the flavor spectrum. Gilles Crochet says that you know what style of wine you will get from the color of the grapes at harvest. "The aromatic complexity of Sauvignon Blanc depends on the color of the skin, which indicates which precursors are present. If it's green it has the precursors for grassy or herbaceous aromatics; if it's yellow the precursors give peach and pear; gold gives mangos and passion fruit."

The transition between terroirs shows at Domaine Vacheron from the steely minerality of silex at Les Romains, to the tight citrus of north-facing limestone at Guigne-Chèvres, to the breadth of lime with stone fruits from the clay-limestone at Chambrates, to stone fruits with apricots from very steep, south-facing limestone at Le Paradis. At one extreme of ripeness, François Cotat is usually one of the last to pick in Chavignol. His Caillottes is perfumed with finesse, Monts Damnés shows mature citrus and gooseberries, Cul de Beaujeu is more open with some apricots flavors, and La Grande Côte has hints of peaches and cream. The terroirs seem to be expressed in nuances of ripeness. Details differ for each producer, but the principle is the same.

Reference Wines for Loire Centre	
Reuilly	Claude Lafond, Le Clos des Messieurs
Quincy	Jean-Michel Sorbe
Menetou-Salon	Henry Pellé, Vignes de Ratier Philippe Gilbert, Les Renardières
Pouilly Fumé	Didier Dagueneau, Blanc de Fumé Jonathan Didier Pabiot, Aubaine
Sancerre	Alphonse Mellot, Les Romains Domaine Vacheron, Les Romains Henri Bourgeois, Monts Damnés Lucien Crochet, Le Chêne François Cotat, Cul de Beaujeu
Sancerre (rosé)	Vincent Pinard Pascal & Nicolas Reverdy
Sancerre (red)	Alphonse Mellot, En Grand Champs Domaine Vacheron, La Belle Dame Henri Bourgeois, La Bourgeoise

The general tendency in Sancerre is to use stainless steel for the basic cuvées, and old oak for the more advanced cuvées, but it may be just as important how long the wine spends on the lees before it is bottled. Tasting in Spring 2014, I saw a great difference depending on which vintage was the current wine at each producer. This was not so much because of the difference between the years, or even the extra age of an older vintage, but the result of the time the wine spends on the lees before bottling. When the current vintage was 2013 it had spent only four months on the lees, whereas when it was 2012 it had spent up to a year before release. The difference was like night and day.

There are top wines matured in either stainless steel or old oak, but to my mind the use of new oak is usually a mistake: when there is sufficient fruit concentration, this can certainly make nice wine, but in the case of Sauvignon Blanc it obscures terroir differences. Sauvignon Blanc may not reflect terroir as obviously as, say, Riesling, but the move towards single vineyard wines in Sancerre highlights the interest of different sites.

Sauvignon Blanc is prized for its freshness and usually consumed young, while it is fresh, delicious, and primary. Many of the single vineyard wines need a little more time: about five years after the vintage is often the perfect point to capture full expression. Sauvignon Blanc will develop further, but with a change of character. A typical aging pattern for top wines is to develop notes of truffles and exotic fruits after about a decade. This is a different style: not everyone will like it, and certainly some wines come off with more subtlety than others, as it can be overpowering.

Red Wine in Sancerre

Sancerre's reputation for crisp, mineral, whites far outshadows the reds (and rosés), but there has been enormous progress in the past two decades with Pinot Noir. The reds used to have a similar reputation to the whites: rather thin and acidic; but today's reds are different. Some wines follow the old tradition of Sancerre, showing light fruits of red cherries with good freshness, and just enough tannin to hold the wine for current drinking. Others have moved in the direction of Burgundy, with dense fruits, often showing precision and good delineation of flavors. The best will easily age for a decade. Producers are quick to say that they are not trying to make Burgundy but Sancerre, but in a blind tasting I would not be surprised if the best wines were confused with the more elegant appellations of the Côte d'Or.

"The consumer desires that red Sancerre is fresh, that it represents the character of the Loire. It's a wine of Spring and Autumn," says Jean-Marie Bourgeois. With this as the stylistic objective, you might think that the wines would not age, but a vertical tasting going back twenty years at Bourgeois shows quite the opposite, with the wines moving in the same savory direction as Burgundy as they age. The cherry fruits of youth become more tertiary, flavors broaden out, and you think about comparisons with the Côte de Beaune.

One sign of the change in emphasis comes from Alphonse Mellot, where a few years back Alphonse fils persuaded his reluctant father to introduce Pinot Noir. Today Alphonse père expresses admiration for his son's foresight, and says forthrightly, "It's difficult to make really good Pinot Noir. If you don't want to reduce your yields to make a top Pinot Noir, you should make a rosé. You can make very nice rosé from Pinot Noir at 80 hl/ha." Tasting through the cuvées, he compares the reds from different vineyards with various parcels of Vosne Romanée. Producing several red cuvées, Alphonse Mellot has taken the lead in Sancerre in demonstrating that Pinot Noir is just as expressive of terroir here as it is in Burgundy. At Vincent Pinard, Clément Pinard shows that Pinot Noir is robust enough to be vinified vendange entière (with the stems). Most of the Pinot Noir in Sancerre is planted on Kimmeridgian terroirs, but Domaine Vacheron is different in focusing its Belle Dame cuvée on siliceous terroir. This brings an elegant, taut quality to the fore, and when you taste the wine, Volnay comes to mind. The last word on the subject goes to Pascal Reverdy: "The image of red Sancerre is the clairet [light red wine], but it's really not true any more."

Vintages

Muscadet

The problem all over northern France in 2016 was a freeze that reduced crop to minimal proportions. 2015 was good in Muscadet and 2014 was excellent (occasionally alcohol levels rose above the usual maximum of 12%), 2013 is decent in spite of some erratic rain at harvest. 2012 was very good in Muscadet, although not in much of the Loire because Muscadet harvested early, just before the rains that spoiled the harvest elsewhere (Muscadet is always the first region to harvest). In Muscadet, Spring was precocious and then cold weather blocked development; there was very small production but nice quality as September gave good maturity. 2011 was complicated by a risk of rot that forced producers to harvest early: alcohol levels are low. "In 2011 it was essential to have manual harvest—the machine harvested grapes were terrible. This is why people say that 2011 was a bad vintage and it got such a poor reputation. But it wasn't so hard if you were able to select your grapes," says Marie Chartier-Luneau. 2010 and 2009 were the recent great vintages: 2009 is the richer, but the risk is that its ripeness makes the wine too rich and fat to be a classic representation of Muscadet. 2008 had a freeze that destroyed a major part of the crop, 2007 was very good, 2006 was average, 2005 was good, 2004 was delicate, 2003 was less affected by the heat wave than elsewhere in France, and 2002 was good.

Anjou and Touraine

The big distinction is between dry wines and sweet wines, in particular whether the weather is good enough after the end of the season for botrytis to occur. Weather has been extremely erratic the past few years. Freeze early in 2016 all but wiped out the harvest, quality is good but yields were low in 2015, 2014 was good with lower yields, but on 2013 the harvest was all but wiped out in Vouvray by hail. In short, 2015 and 2014 are a pair of magical years; the wines of 2014 may perhaps last a bit longer. 2012 was a very difficult year for all wines because of rain: there was almost no sweet wine, and most whites were dry. "In 2012 we were forced to harvest before the rain. We made only three dry wines, one Sec from each property," says Hugo Hwang at Domaine Huët. Conditions were the opposite in 2011, which was too dry for much botrytis: most sweet wines are passerillé, but the dry wines are quite good.

The previous years, 2010 and 2009 offer an interesting contrast. As typified by Savennières, but in the Loire generally, 2009 was a rounder year that has more extract and less minerality, generally rich (although not as much as 2005 or 2003). If you really want to see the typicity of Chenin Blanc, it is clearer in 2010. For sweet wines, 2010 offered good development of botrytis. "2009 was a glorious year; every producer was able to decide what they wanted to produce," says Hugo Hwang. For the reds, the extra heat of 2009 produced a richness that is not so obvious in 2010, but Yannick Amirault in Bourgueil says, "The 2010 was for me the great vintage, better than 2009. 2010 is perhaps less gourmand but it has good acidity." At Couly-Dutheil, Jacques Couly says that, "2010 is an aristocratic vintage, but 2009 has richness."

2008 was a difficult year and many wines have vegetal aromas. Although there were sweet wines produced in 2008, they suffer from the same vegetal impression as the dry wines. 2007 was a powerful vintage, perhaps too much so, for dry wines, but made rich sweet wines and ripe red wines. Previously 2005 and 2003 were the richest vintages.

Sancerre & Pouilly Fumé

2015 was an early vintage of very high quality (picking started in Sancerre around the same time as Muscadet), and 2014 was as good as elsewhere in the Loire. The 2013 vintage was surprisingly good in the Centre, given difficulties all across France; the wines are lively and fresh. "We were very worried about 2013 but pleasantly surprised at fermentation. The wines have come out well," says Nathalie Lafond. Rain was the difficulty in 2012 but the wines have retained good fruit and freshness. In the end, this is a rich vintage; producers are especially pleased with their Pinot Noirs. "2012 is one of the best vintages for Pinot Noir, it is really ripe, but it is not heavy, it's fresh and elegant," says Clément Pinard.

The precocious vintage of 2011 has given wines with less obvious fruit than 2012 that are attractive in the short to mid term. The difference between 2010 and 2009 is the same as elsewhere: 2010 is more classic, leaner and fresher, while 2009 tends to opulence. Cool wet conditions of 2008 produced wines with high acidity, often developing rapidly; 2007 started in similar fashion but was rescued by a good autumn.

Rain at harvest in 2006 spoiled many wines, and any left are probably now too old. 2005 was an excellent vintage; only the best whites are still interesting, but the reds are just coming into their own. 2004 was too rainy, and 2003 was too hot. 2002 was a classic vintage; the whites have now turned from freshness to truffles, but the top reds are just about right.

	2016	2015	2014	2013	2012	2011	2010
Muscadet		**	***		***		***
Anjou/Touraine white		***	***			**	***
Anjou sweet white		***	**			*	***
Anjou/Touraine red		***	***			*	**
Centre		**	***	*	**	*	**

	2009	2008	2007	2006	2005	2004	2003	2002	2001
Muscadet	**	*	**		**	*	*	***	**
Anjou/Touraine white	**		**		**	*	*		
Anjou sweet white	***		**		***		**		
Anjou/Touraine red	***		**		***	*	**	**	*
Centre	**		*		***		*	***	*

Profiles of Estates

Ratings	
***	Excellent producers defining the very best of the appellation
**	Top producers whose wines typify the appellation
*	Very good producers making wines of character that rarely disappoint

Symbols

 Address

 Phone

 Person to contact

 Email

 Website

 Principal AOP

 IGP

 Red   Rosé   White   Sweet   Sparkling   Reference wines

 Grower-producer

 Negociant (or purchases grapes)

 Cooperative

 Lutte raisonnée (sustainable viticulture)

 Organic

 Biodynamic

 Tastings/visits possible

 By appointment only

 No visits

 Sales directly at producer

No direct sales

ha = estate vineyards; bottles = annual production

Muscadet

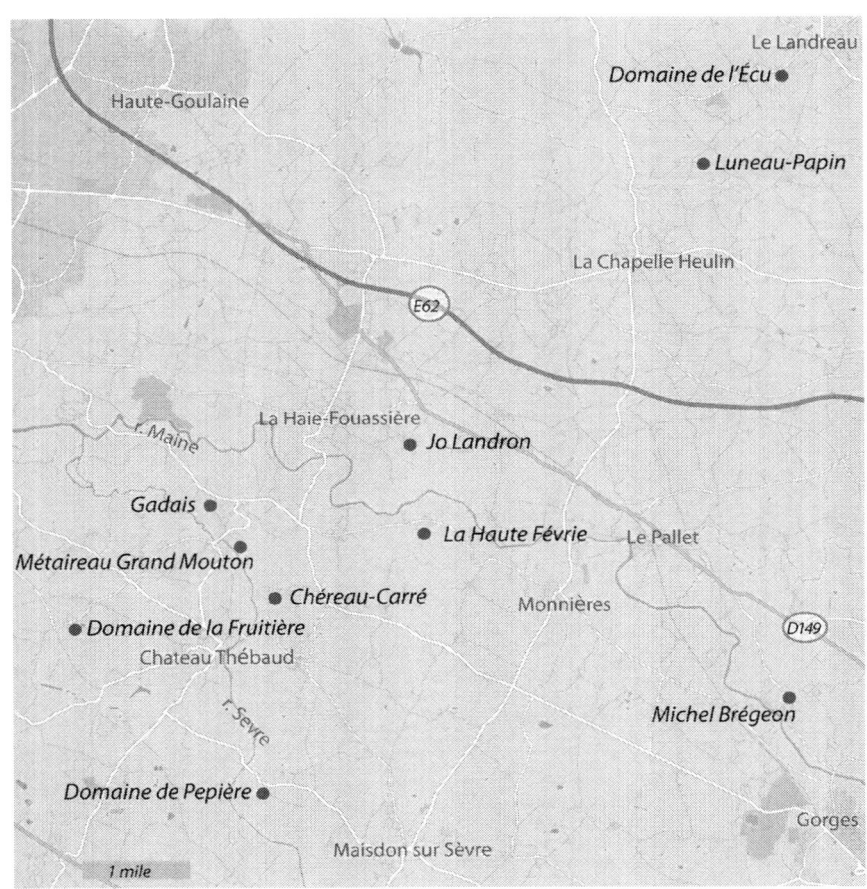

Michel Brégeon

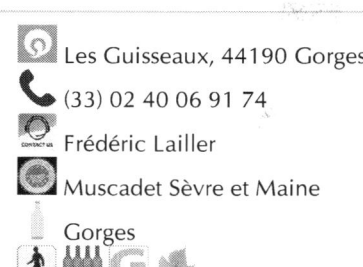 Les Guisseaux, 44190 Gorges

(33) 02 40 06 91 74

Frédéric Lailler

Muscadet Sèvre et Maine

Gorges

9 ha; 35,000 bottles

Committed to improving the quality of Muscadet, Michel Brégeon believes the region should focus on a smaller overall appellation area with a hierarchy of the best terroirs. He was involved in establishing the Gorges Cru, for which his wine is regarded as a flagship, coming from the classic terroir of gabbro (a basalt-like rock). His Muscadet Sèvre et Maine also comes from gabbro terroir. From 2014 there is also a cuvée from Clisson; "we exchanged some vines with someone who didn't have Gorges," Michel explains, "we didn't buy new vines." Michel established the estate in 1975 with just 3 ha when he left the family domain, then he inherited some additional vines from his father in 1989. His protégé Frédéric Lailler took over when Michel retired in 2011, but Michel stays involved, joining the tasting when I visited the domain. Vinification is traditional: grapes go straight into the press, the must is only partially clarified, fermentation is by natural yeasts, and the domain is known for keeping wines on the lees for longer than usual, sometimes for several years, in glass-lined cuves underground. "When you keep the wine aging longer, you lose the primary aromas. but the terroir begins to express itself, and you see the particularité of Gorges," Michel says. The style emphasizes purity of fruits, often with a fresh uplift at the end, and the wines have definite age worthiness. A vertical tasting of the Muscadet sur lie suggests the peak is reached around three years after the vintage. Fred Lailler believes the wine is just right after 18 months in the bottle, and he regrets that the wine tends to go into distribution for sale sooner. Gorges ages longer, peaking around 6 years after release (usually it is aged for 40 months); it is always flavorful. The 2004, which was bottled in 2010, seemed just to have reached its peak in 2016. Clisson comes from granite terroir, and is more mineral, and deeper, but may not age quite as long.

Domaine Chéreau Carré

🌀 Domaine de Chasseloir, 44690 Saint Fiacre-sur-Maine

📞 (33) 02 40 54 81 15

@ contact@chereau-carre.fr

Patrick Macé

🌐 www.chereau-carre.fr

⬤ Muscadet Sèvre et Maine

Château de l'Oiselinière, Le Clos

🚶 🏭 G

100 ha; 700,000 bottles

An old family in the region, Chéreau Carré expanded in the 1960s-1970s. Today it is one of the larger independent producers of Muscadet, with four separate properties: Château de Chasseloir, Château l'Oiselinière, Château de la Chesnaie, and Domaine du Bois Bruley. All production is sur lie. There is manual harvesting, 48 hours maceration, and vinification with natural yeast: the general concern is to preserve fruit as long as possible. Wine is kept on the lees with battonage every two weeks for six months for the Cuvée Classique, longer for special cuvées, up to 15 months. Stainless steel is used except for a special cuvée that is vinified entirely in barriques of new oak (labeled as *vinifié en fûts de chêne neufs*). Château de Chasseloir is the most important holding, with most vines more than 40 years old, and a small parcel of 100-year-old vines that makes the Comte Leloup Cuvée des Ceps Centenaires. The original vines were planted on rootstocks, but since then have been propagated by marcottage (sticking shoots in the ground to form new roots). The other old vines bottling is Le Clos du Château l'Oiselinière from terroir of orthogneiss. At the other extreme, there is a bottling from young vines called La Griffe Bernard Chéreau. The style here varies with the cuvée, from straightforward with the basic Muscadet Sèvre et Maine of each property, to the greater structure of the old vines bottlings, and the somewhat overwhelming oak of the cuvée in new wood.

Domaine de l'Écu ★★

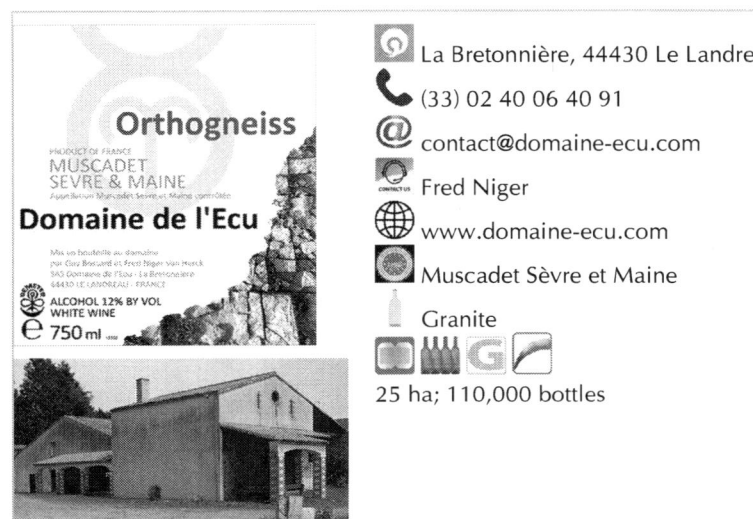

La Bretonnière, 44430 Le Landreau

(33) 02 40 06 40 91

contact@domaine-ecu.com

Fred Niger

www.domaine-ecu.com

Muscadet Sèvre et Maine

Granite

25 ha; 110,000 bottles

"He's a vrai de vrai," someone who knows the wine scene well in the Loire said when they heard I was visiting Guy Bossard at Domaine de l'Ecu, which I suppose is as good a way as any of saying that Guy is the real thing. Indeed he is... Guy makes proper wines with a tendency towards the savory rather than the aromatic. Even the Cuvée Classique, the general assemblage from young vines (young here means less than 35 years), shows minerality. The domain has vineyards on three terroirs, gneiss, orthogneiss, and granite, which are the basis for individual cuvées from older vines (40-45 years). The style is precise, mineral and stony, offering insights into the typicity of the variety and its response to terroir. All wines are matured in cuves in the traditional way, bringing out the purity of fruits, with minimal intervention, including very low sulfur. The Cuvée Classique stays on the lees for 10 months, the three terroir bottlings for 15-18 months. The domain was one of the first to take up biodynamic viticulture. The latest cuvée is the Taurus bottling, which is matured in old fûts (barriques in some years). The inspiration for Taurus came from Guy's partner, Fred Niger, who came into the domain two years ago. You would expect nothing less than a top result from Guy Brossard, but somehow I have the feeling that his heart isn't in this in the same way as in the terroir-driven series. There is also a sparkling wine, La Divina, made from an assemblage of several varieties.

Domaine de La Fruitière

La Fruitière, La Croix de la Bourdinière, 44690 Château Thébaud

(33) 02 40 06 53 05

contact@lieubeau.com

François & Vincent Lieubeau

www.lieubeau.com

Muscadet Sèvre et Maine

Château de la Bourdinière, Prestige

80 ha; 500,000 bottles

"We may have seven generations of winemakers, but in fact my father did everything," says François Lieubeau. "Two generations ago my grandfather had 7 ha." Today there are 60 ha spread over four properties in Muscadet, and another 20 ha for IGP. In Muscadet the properties are Château de la Bourdinière (granite), Château de la Placelière (granite), Château de l'Aulnaye (gneiss in Château-Thébaud), and Domaine de la Fruitière (varying terroirs). One of the largest producers in the region, Lieubeau was one of the first to plant Chardonnay (mostly sold under the Lieubeau label). "We have very good terroir in the Pays Nantais and Chardonnay is well adapted to it," François says. The Chardonnay and IGP Sauvignon Blanc sell at around the same price as the entry-level Muscadet. Wines are all aged in cuve, using glass lined underground tanks (traditional here) or stainless steel. The style shows significant variation from the entry level wines to the cuvées or crus. Entry level wines are made in a fruit-forward, crowd-pleasing style, whether Muscadet or varietal-labeled IGP Val de Loire. The more advanced wines split between a fairly traditional Prestige cuvée from Château de la Bourdinière or the Château Thébaud Cru from Château de l'Aulnaye, and the more "international" M de la Fruitière, which exceptionally uses both oak and malolactic fermentation. There is clearly an intention to pay some attention to the demands of the market.

Domaine Gadais Père et Fils

Gadais Père et Fils, Saint Fiacre-Sur-Maine

33 (0)2 40 54 81 23

musgadais@wanadoo.fr

Christophe Gadais

www.gadaispereetfils.fr

Muscadet Sèvre et Maine

Muscadet Sèvre et Maine, Vieilles Vignes

52 ha; 360,000 bottles

Christophe Gadais is the fifth generation of winemakers in the family; after a stint in Sancerre, he took over the domain in 1994. Vineyards are in the commune of St. Fiacre, where they are divided into 120 small parcels. "We are in the heart of the appellation and there are five cuvées; each comes from a different set of parcels," Christophe says. A good sense of structure runs through the wines, which are solid representations of Muscadet. Except for the simple Muscadet, Emotions, which comes from young vines near Vertou, all the wines are sur lie. Even the entry level Domaine de La Tourmaline has a savory sense of structure rather than simple aromatics. The Vieilles Vignes (from a vineyard originally planted in 1929) shows a definite texture coming from the lees, and the Les Perrières monopole (from a parcel planted by Christophe's father in the 1950s, but produced as a separate cuvée for the first time in 2009) is matured half in oak to give a broader style. Gadais is one of the few producers in Muscadet who have tried screwcaps (principally for export). Does this change the wine? "I don't know, but it depends what you expect of aging, do you want the wine to change its taste?" Christophe says. The wines will remain labeled as Muscadet Sèvre et Maine, as the name of the Cru covering Gadais's vineyards is Monnières St. Fiacre. "The name of the cru is too complicated and difficult to explain, I'm not going to use it," is Christophe's view.

Domaine du Grand Mouton

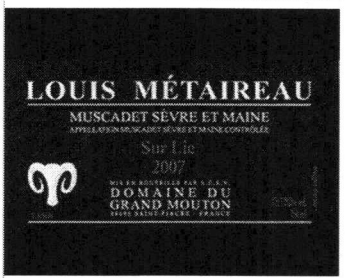

 Le Gue Joubert, 44690 Maisdon-sur-Sèvre

📞 (33) 02 40 54 81 92

@ contact@muscadet-grandmouton.com

 Marie-Luce Metaireau

🌐 www.muscadet-grandmouton.com

Muscadet Sèvre et Maine

Grand Mouton

30 ha

Grand Mouton is located on a rise in the middle of the region between the rivers Sèvre and Maine. The winery is surrounded by a parcel of 23 ha and there are a further 7 ha in two other villages. Terroir is mostly gneiss with various kinds of mica. The oldest vines go back to 1937, when Grand Mouton was planted. Most vines are now around 40 years old. There are 3-4 cuvées depending on the year. Petit Mouton is the young vines cuvée (although young vines here might be Vieilles Vignes elsewhere); Grand Mouton is the major bottling. MLM comes from a small plot established in 1933 on the other side of the village, just above the river. Cuvée #1 comes from the oldest vines in Grand Mouton, planted in 1937 at the foot of the hill; it is made only in the best vintages. Wines spend 7-9 months on the lees. The general style here brings freshness to the forefront, although the wines become perceptibly more powerful as you move from the first cuvées to MLM and then to Cuvée #1. The style can be quite reserved when young, with flavor variety broadening out around three years after the vintage. The wines usually show a fine structure. They do not like high alcohol here. "It's one of our aims to start the harvest as soon as possible; usually we are the earliest to start in Muscadet. Sometimes there is a cuvée called 10.5, named for the (low) percent of alcohol. It's difficult to get grapes ripe enough at 10.5% but we like to do it when we can," says Marie-Luce Métaireau.

Domaine La Haute Févrie

DOMAINE LA HAUTE FÉVRIE

Muscadet Sèvre et Maine
APPELLATION MUSCADET SÈVRE ET MAINE CONTRÔLÉE
Sur Lie

PRODUCE DE FRANCE

12% vol.
750 ml   Mis en bouteilles au Domaine

PAR CLAUDE BRANGER, VIGNERON RÉCOLTANT, LA FÉVRIE, 44690 MAISDON SUR SÈVRE, FRANCE
TEL 02 40 36 94 08

La Fevrie, Maisdon-sur-Sèvre, 44690

(33) 02 40 36 94 08

contact@lahautefevrie.com

Claude et Sébastien Branger

www.lahautefevrie.com

Muscadet Sèvre et Maine

Cuvée Excellence

21 ha; 70,000 bottles

Located in the village of Maisdon-sur-Sèvre, the domain has a beautiful house and garden with a practical cellar underneath. Claude Branger now works with his son Sébastien, who represents the fourth generation. Vineyards are in several parcels, spread out all around the village, mostly in plots of 3-4 ha. Viticulture is mostly lutte raisonnée, although 9 ha have been converted to organic. There are several cuvées of Muscadet (all but one are sur lie), defined by terroir or the age of the vines. The domain wine comes from 35-year-old vines; Moulin de la Gustais is from 50-year-old vines; and Cuvée Excellence is from 50- to 80-year-old vines first planted in 1922. There are also cuvées from specific terroirs: Gras Moutons (from an area of amphibolite between the rivers Sèvre and Maine) and the Cru Monnières St. Fiacre. All of these are vinified and matured in cuve, but there is one further cuvée, Clos Joubert, produced in small amounts, using a mixture of acacia and oak barriques. There are also sparkling and late harvest wines. The entry-level cuvées spend 6-8 months on the lees, the top cuvées spend 15-16 months, and the crus spend 21 months. The style here is very round and fruity for Muscadet. Young wines can verge on spicy, with earthy hints of sweet tobacco, which become accentuated as the wine ages. This richer style of Muscadet shows potential for aging, as I have had wines of more than a decade's age (back to 1999) that still remain lively.

Domaines Joseph Landron

AMPHIBOLITE
NATURE

M U S C A D E T
Appellation Muscadet Contrôlée

3 Impasse Fief du Breil, La Haie Fouassière, 44690

(33) 02 40 54 83 27

@ domaines.landron@wanadoo.fr

Joseph Landron

www.domaines-landron.com

Muscadet Sèvre et Maine

Amphibolite

50 ha; 300,000 bottles

Joseph Landron's father started with his brother in 1945 with a couple of hectares. He expanded the estate and formed a group of vignerons to sell wine direct. Joseph joined in 1979 and expanded the business further. Today there are two domains, Le Château de la Carizière and Domaine de la Louvetrie. When his father retired, he started to reduce yields. "The aim is to make a natural wine. I was reacting against the situation with yields that were too high, chaptalization, etc.," he says. After an accident that poisoned some vines, Joseph moved to organic and then biodynamic viticulture. Today there are six cuvées, and also a sparkling wine and a tiny production of Vin de France. Vinification by terroir started with one exceptional parcel, but since 1982 everything has been vinified by parcel. Three cuvées are based on terroirs reflecting different types of soils: quartz, orthogneiss, amphibolite; one cuvée is an assemblage. Cuvée Tradition comes from clay soils, and is treated differently. "This is the only cuvée that I allow myself to vinify in oak," Jo says. With an eye for modern marketing, the name of Jo Landron is more important than the names of the individual domains. The wines give an impression of being well balanced for immediate consumption, although one or two older wines showed better aging potential than might be suggested by current vintages. A common sense of restraint on the nose translates into an impression of delicacy on the palate; acidity and fruits are rarely aggressive.

Domaine Pierre Luneau-Papin ★★

🔘 Domaine de La Grange, Le Landreau, 44430

📞 (33) 02 40 06 45 27

@ domaineluneaupapin@wanadoo.fr

👤 Marie Chartier Luneau

🌐 www.domaineluneaupapin.com

🍇 Muscadet Sèvre et Maine

🍾 Muscadet Sèvre et Maine, L d'Or

🚶 🏭 G 🍷

35 ha; 220,000 bottles

"Ah, that will be a long visit," they said at other domains when they heard I was visiting Luneau-Papin. Indeed it was. Marie Chartier-Luneau, Pierre Papin's daughter-in-law, bubbles over with contagious enthusiasm, not merely for the domain but also for the appellation. She makes a fine ambassador for Muscadet. Created in 1990, the domain took its name from the marriage of Monique Luneau to Pierre Papin (both from old winegrowing families). With many small parcels, the focus is on terroir, with eight cuvées from Muscadet distinguished by different terroirs and vine age. Vinification is similar for all. "Everything is done in cuve. We have no oak, no barriques, no MLF, no chaptalization. Yields vary from 25-45 hl/ha depending on the age of the vines. Time spent on the lees is the only variable aside from the terroir. There is battonage in the spring after harvest, but otherwise we close the tank and wait until bottling," says Pierre-Marie Luneau. The cuvées include: Pierre de la Grange, from mica-schist; Clos des Allées, from 50-year old vines on mica-schist near the winery; Les Pierres Blanche, from 55-year-old vines on gneiss near Chapelle-Heulin; "L" d'Or, from 35-year-old vines on granite; Terre de Pierre, from 35-year-old vines on serpentine rock; and the top cuvée, Excelsior, from 80-year old vines on mica-schist in the area of the Goulaine Cru, which is given three years on the lees. The wines are splendid examples of modern Muscadet.

Domaine de La Pépière ★★

44690 Maisdon-sur-Sèvre

02 40 03 81 19

contact@domainedelapepiere.com

Marc Ollivier & Remi Branger & Gwenaelle Croix

www.domainedelapepiere.com

Muscadet Sèvre et Maine

Clisson

35 ha; 200,000 bottles

This widely acclaimed domain was started in 1984 by Marc Ollivier and Remi Branger with 8 ha. Today it has 30 ha of Muscadet and 5 ha for making IGP Val de Loire red. The winery is a ramshackle looking group of buildings in the woods just outside Maisdon-sur-Sèvre. Cuvées are based on terroir. Gras Mouton comes from gneiss and spend 7 months on the lees. Clos des Briords comes from 60-year-old vines on granite similar to Château-Thébaud, and spends 7 months on the lees. Clos Cormerais comes from vines planted after 1927, on east-facing clay-silex, and is the only cuvée matured in wood (in a mixture of oak and acacia barriques: "We're not looking for the taste of oak, just for oxygen exposure," Rémi says). Clisson spends 24 months on the lees; Château-Thébaud Clos des Morins spends 30 months on the lees; and Cuvée #3 is named for its three years in the cuve. There's battonage more or less once a year. The house style shows finesse. There's a refinement and elegance to the cuvées from Muscadet Sèvre et Maine, with the same style taken to greater intensity by the wines from the Crus and Cuvée #3 (an assemblage from Clisson and Château-Thébaud that provides a perfect compromise between the two Crus and makes a strong case for blending). As refined as Muscadet comes, the wines have a precision of fruits that is unusual for the appellation, and a definite sense of ageworthiness. They are among the top wines of Muscadet.

Anjou

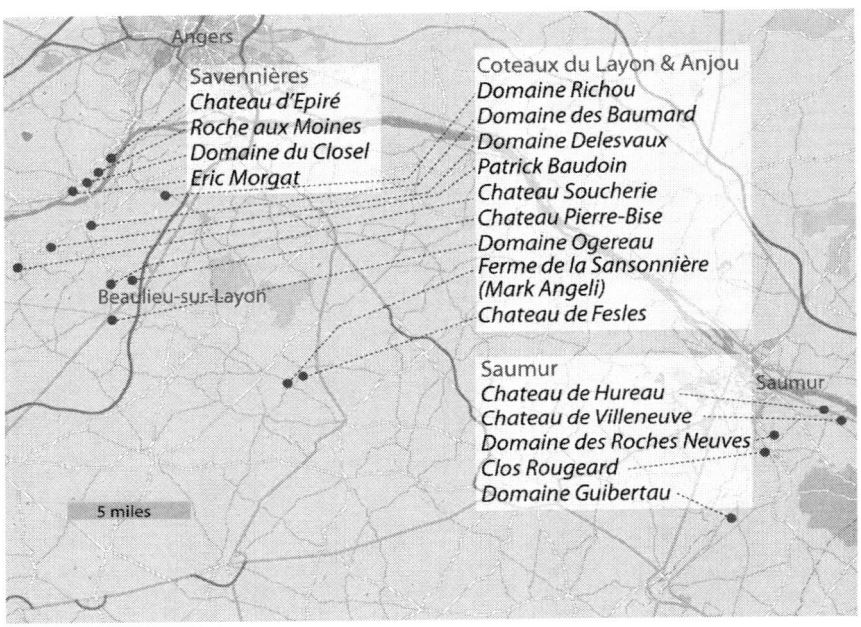

Angers

Savennières
Chateau d'Epiré
Roche aux Moines
Domaine du Closel
Eric Morgat

Coteaux du Layon & Anjou
Domaine Richou
Domaine des Baumard
Domaine Delesvaux
Patrick Baudoin
Chateau Soucherie
Chateau Pierre-Bise
Domaine Ogereau
Ferme de la Sansonnière
(Mark Angeli)
Chateau de Fesles

Beaulieu-sur-Layon

Saumur
Chateau de Hureau
Chateau de Villeneuve
Domaine des Roches Neuves
Clos Rougeard
Domaine Guibertau

Saumur

5 miles

Domaine Patrick Baudouin

Princé, 49290 Chaudefonds-sur-Layon

(33) 02 41 78 66 04

contact@patrick-baudouin-layon.com

Patrick Baudouin

www.patrick-baudouin-layon.com

Coteaux du Layon

Savennières

Coteaux du Layon, Les Buandières

15 ha; 45,000 bottles

Patrick Baudouin started out as a Maoist with revolutionary intentions and has strong views on the appellation system and the true character of Loire wines. The domain was founded in 1920 by his great grandparents, and he returned to Anjou in 1990 to take it over. It remains a small domain, in which Patrick is assisted by his nephew. His original intention was to make sweet wines in the Coteaux du Layon. but compelled by vintage conditions, Patrick made his first dry wine in 2000, and in 2001 started regular production of dry wines. Today the domain has 10 ha of Chenin Blanc and 3 ha of Cabernet Franc; the main holdings are in Quarts de Chaume. "My belief is that my dry wines should be true dry wines at 13% or 14% without botrytis," he now says. All wines are matured in wood, using a mixture of barriques and demi-muids. Patrick divides his wines into 'vins de fruit' and 'vins de terroir.' There's a small negociant business (Patrick Baudouin Vins) that produces Anjou Rouge and Blanc, but the main interest comes with the domain wines from specific parcels. Effusion is a cuvée of Anjou Blanc from young vines and offers the most direct fruit impressions; the Anjou Blanc La Cornillard comes from old vines and has something of the minerality of the Savennières, which comes from a hectare the estate planted in 2009. The red Anjou Coteaux d'Ardenay is an assemblage of Cabernet Franc and Cabernet Sauvignon, the amount of the latter depending on the year. Patrick remains best known for his sweet wines, which increase in intensity from the young vines Coteaux du Layon (coming from a plot close to Quarts to Chaume), to the cuvée Les Buandières, and Quarts de Chaume.

Domaine Baumard **

8, rue de l'Abbaye 49190 Rochefort-sur-Loire

(33) 02 41 78 70 03

info@baumard.fr

Florent Baumard

www.baumard.fr

Coteaux du Layon

Savennières, Clos du Papillon

Quarts de Chaume

35 ha; 180,000 bottles

This is a leading domain for both dry and sweet wines, created by Florent Baumard's father, although the family have been winegrowers for generations. The estate has 50 ha, with 35 ha in production. The top dry wine comes from Savennières, where Baumard owns half of the famous Clos du Papillon; it displays the savory minerality that characterizes Chenin Blanc at its best. There is also the Clos Saint-Yves monopole and Trie Spéciale, a Savennières AOP produced only in some years by successive harvests, often with some botrytis. Baumard's style tends to richness, especially as you progress from Savennières AOP to the Clos du Papillon to the Trie Spéciale. These are very fine wines. However, the domain is best known for its sweet wines. From the Coteaux du Layon, Carte d'Or is a selection from many parcels, Clos de Sainte Catherine comes from a specific north-facing schist terroir, and cuvée Le Payon represents selection from the same parcels as Carte d'Or but at the same quality level as Sainte Catherine. The top sweet wine comes from the Quarts de Chaume and is a peak example of the botrytized style; although there is controversy about Baumard's use of cryoselection, the wine speaks for itself: concentrated, delicious, honeyed, and long. In addition to the white wines, Baumard produces Anjou red, rosé, and Crémant, and also Vin de France, including the Vert de l'Or that is a play on the name of Verdelho, a grape variety from Madeira that used to be grown in the Loire.

Domaine du Closel

Château-des-Vaults, 1 place du Mail, 49170 Savennières

📞 (33) 02 41 72 81 00

@ evelyne@savennieres-closel.com

Evelyne de Pontbriand

🌐 www.savennieres-closel.com

Savennières

Savennières, Clos du Papillon

16 ha; 50,000 bottles

The rather grand château is located right in the town square. "This is a typical property for Anjou of the nineteenth century, with a château and park leading to the vineyard," says Evelyne de Pontbriand. One of the largest properties in Savennières, the domain notably owns half of the Clos du Papillon. A change to a richer style occurred in the early 2000s, with ripeness assessed by phenolic rather than alcoholic maturity. Three cuvées from Savennières are harvested at different times to produce different effects. La Jalousie is harvested from the youngest vines when the berries are still yellow, to give direct, forward fruits. Les Caillardières comes from the top of the hill and is harvested when the berries are a little browner to produce a fuller result; the wine has more obvious Chenin typicity. Clos du Papillon is harvested last with very ripe berries, which may even include some botrytis. The first two are matured in cuve, the Papillon in 2- to 3-year-old barriques. The domain was certified organic in 2006, and is biodynamic today. House style varies because the vintage is allowed to express itself—MLF may or may not occur, although usually it does not—but the common thread is a sheen of glycerin through which come the characteristic cereal, nuts, and savory notes of Chenin Blanc. Depending on vintage, wines may vary from precise as in 2010 to the broader impression of 2009. Like proprietor Evelyne de Pontbriand, they are always elegant and interesting.

Domaine Delesvaux **

Les Essards, La Haie Longue, 49190 Saint Aubin de Luigné

(33) 02 41 78 18 71

dom.delesvaux.philippe@wanadoo.fr

Catherine & Philippe Delesvaux

Coteaux du Layon

Anjou, l'Authenthique

Les Clos

11 ha; 30,000 bottles

When Catherine and Philippe Delesvaux met, he was practicing polyculture in Chaudefonds-sur-Layon, but wanted to focus on wine. They started the domain in 1978 with 1 ha, and built it up to 3 ha, but Catherine continued as a teacher until 1997. They moved to St. Aubin when their present vineyards became available to rent; and then they were able to purchase them six years ago. By making some exchanges, they now have a contiguous domain, divided into several vineyards. "We are the first generation, and the domain is small because there are only two of us," Catherine says. The winery is a practical warehouse building in the middle of the vines. The domain lies between the Loire and Layon valleys and specializes in sweet wines from the Coteaux du Layon, but there are also dry white wines under the Anjou appellation and varietal Cabernet Franc (Le Roc) and Cabernet Sauvignon (La Montée de l'Epine). Three quarters of plantings are Chenin Blanc. "Everything is natural here," says Catherine: there are no added yeasts or chaptalization, very little sulfur, and maturation for the whites in old barriques, with battonage when necessary. Reds have élevage in tank. When the vintage permits, three cuvées of Coteaux du Layon are distinguished by levels of botrytis in multiple passes through the vineyard. "At harvest we select the botrytized grapes first for the SGN cuvée; the second selection is for Le Clos with a 50:50 mixture of botrytized and over-mature berries; and then the last trie is for over-mature berries for the Passerillé cuvée," Catherine explains. Sometimes there is an ultimate selection of super-botrytized grapes, called l'Anthologie, but this has been made only four times. (But in 2012, 2013, and 2104 there was only a single sweet wine. "We don't add sugar to sweet wine," says Catherine, "if sugar is not high enough we prefer not to make the wine.") Even the very rich fully botrytized desert wines continue to show purity of fruits. The two Anjou Blancs make an interesting comparison. They come from two 1 ha plots (within the Coteaux du Layon AOP), but are used to make dry wine (sec-tendre in some vintages). Feuille d'Or comes from vines grafted on rootstocks in the conventional way, while Cuvée Authentique comes from a plot of ungrafted vines across the road (planted in 2000 on previously uncultivated land). Why plant ungrafted vines? "It was a challenge, as specialists in Chenin, we wanted to find the true flavor of Chenin Blanc before phylloxera. It's not very economic, the yields are very low." The ungrafted vines give yields of 6-12 hl/ha, whereas the plot on rootstocks gives yields of 15-20 hl/ha. While Feuille d'Or is very good, Cuvée Authentique lifts Chenin Blanc to a new level of intensity

Château d'Epiré

49170 Savennières

(33) 02 41 77 15 01

luc.bizard@wanadoo.fr

Luc Bizard

www.chateau-epire.com

Savennières

Savennières, Cuvée Spéciale

11 ha; 45,000 bottles

The winery is located in the old church of Epiré, just across from the rather splendid nineteenth century château (which is no longer part of the vineyard estate). Luc Bizard inherited the vineyards, where the largest parcel, Le Parc, located just behind the château, was planted in 1969. Terroir is mostly schist, but quite heterogeneous. Viticulture is conventional, but yields have been going down. "Yields are usually 35-45 hl/ha; 25 years ago they were 45-50 hl/ha. I reduced yields to make richer wine, but now we are on the other side, the wines can be too rich and alcoholic," Luc says. There are three principal dry cuvées and (depending on the vintage) sometimes wines in sweet styles (usually moelleux). There is no single style here because the three dry cuvées are all quite different. The mainstream Savennières is the Château d'Epiré, fermented and matured in cuve. Cuvée Spéciale comes from a 1 ha parcel with an unusual terroir of black stones, just south of the Château. This is fermented and matured in old barriques. Made since 2000, Hu-Boyau comes from the oldest part of the vineyard, and is barrel fermented with complete MLF; there are 7-8 barrels (one of which is new). "Here we make a wine for the international taste," Luc explains. The richness overwhelms the typicity of Chenin Blanc (which to my palate shows more clearly on the Cuvée Special). There's also an entry-level wine with a touch of residual sugar (Cuvée E) and an Anjou red.

Château de Fesles

GRAND VIN DE LOIRE

CHÂTEAU
DE FESLES
Bonnezeaux
Chenin

Bernard Germain   2005

49380 Thouarcé

(33) 02 41 68 94 02

sauvion@sauvion.fr

Gilles Bigot

www.fesles.com

Coteaux du Layon

Bonnezeaux

55 ha; 270,000 bottles

The château is an impressive building set in lovely grounds, surrounded by vineyards. Château de Fesles was bought by the major negociant Les Grands Chais de France in 2008, and the sparkling new cuves of stainless steel show that there has obviously been much investment. 35 ha of the holdings are immediately around the château, which is on the edge of Bonnezeaux, where they own 14 ha (schist terroir, all planted with Chenin Blanc), which makes Château de Fesles the largest owner of Bonnezeaux. The château is on a high point so there are constant winds, which prolong the growing season. In addition to Chenin Blanc on the slopes, Cabernet Franc and Cabernet Sauvignon are planted on the gravel plateau for Anjou red, and there is also some Grolleau and Gamay for the Anjou rosé. The style is workmanlike. The bottlings from Anjou are all good examples of the various styles; the rosé d'Anjou is more to my palate than the Cabernet d'Anjou; the whites show Chenin character and the reds show Cabernet Franc character. The highlight here is of course the Bonnezeaux. "We make one cuvée of Bonnezeaux, which is the best we can make. Basically the Bonnezeaux is a selection and anything that does not make the cut is declassified to Coteaux du Layon," says winemaker Gilles Bigot. In 2012 there was no Bonnezeaux, as it was all declassified to Coteaux du Layon, but the 2010 is far and away the best example of Bonnezeaux in recent years.

Domaine Guiberteau **

 Mollay, 3 Impasse du Cabernet, 49260 Saint Just-sur-Dive

📞 (33) 02 41 38 78 94

@ domaine.guiberteau@wanadoo.fr

 Romain Guiberteau

🌐 www.domaineguiberteau.fr

◉ Saumur

🍷 Saumur Blanc, Domaine

10 ha; 45,000 bottles

Founded at the start of the twentieth century, the domain was greatly extended in 1954 by the purchase of 7 ha on the famous hill of Brézé just south of Saumur. However, the vineyards were leased out in 1976 when no one in the family wanted to take over the estate. It was revived in 1996 when Romain Guiberteau decided to take back the leases and manage the domain. His first vintage was guided by Dani Foucault of Clos Rougeard; since then Romain has increasingly put his stamp on the domain. Divided between Chenin Blanc and Cabernet Franc, plantings include vines up to eighty years old. Besides Brézé, there are smaller vineyards (a hectare each) nearby at Bizet and Montreil-Bellay. There are four white wines and three reds. The influence of Clos Rougeard shows in the purity of style. Le Domaine is the introductory wine in both red and white, coming from younger vines and matured without oak exposure since 2009. Then in whites there are Clos de Guichaux (a blend from the youngest vines in Bizay and Brézé), Brézé (a blend from two parcels of 50-year-old vines on clay-limestone terroir, matured in a mix of new, one-year, and two-year barriques), and Clos des Carmes (from a recently replanted plot in a clos dating from the eleventh century that's considered to have the best terroir in Brézé). The two single vineyard reds are Les Motelles (from a 1 ha plot of sandier soil at Montreil-Bellay) and Les Arboises (from a small south-facing parcel on the hill of Brézé).

Château de Hureau

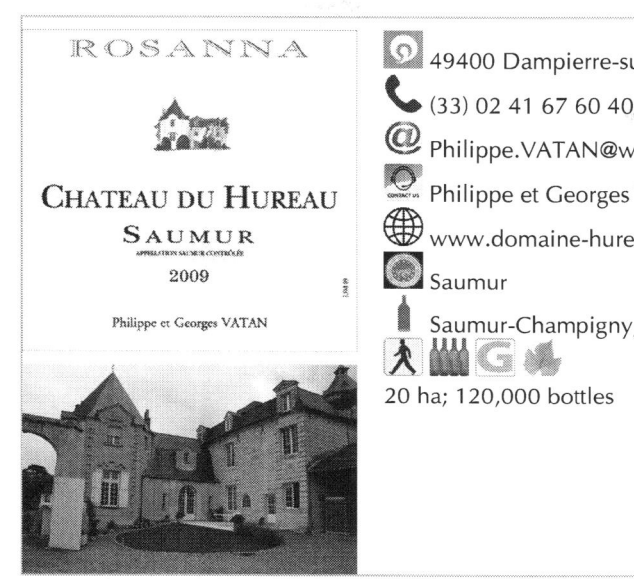

ROSANNA

CHATEAU DU HUREAU

SAUMUR
APPELLATION SAUMUR CONTRÔLÉE
2009

Philippe et Georges VATAN

49400 Dampierre-sur-Loire

(33) 02 41 67 60 40

Philippe.VATAN@wanadoo.fr

Philippe et Georges Vatan

www.domaine-hureau.fr

Saumur

Saumur-Champigny, Four à Chaux

20 ha; 120,000 bottles

Located at the edge of the Saumur-Champigny appellation, close to the Loire, the château dates from the eighteenth century, with an impressive octagonal tower, but has thirteenth century caves carved out beneath from the underlying tufa rock. The focus is on red wines, exclusively Cabernet Franc, but there's also a little dry white, and in exceptional years a liquoreux. About 3 ha of vineyards are in a flat parcel above the Château, but the rest are broken up into many small parcels in Dampierre. The subsoil is tufa, with variations in the top soil showing a typical mix of clay and calcareous soils for the region. Most (90%) plantings are Cabernet Franc. The style brings out minerality and showcases purity of fruit. The red cuvées come from different terroirs, and vary in their balance of overt fruit to structure. Fours à Chaux is perhaps the most direct (coming from sand and tufa, which gives a fine structure), Lisagathe is the purest (from just above the Château, where 60-year-old vines grow on clay soil), and Les Fevettes (from deeper soils) shows the broadest flavor spectrum. Proprietor Philippe Vatan, who took over in 1987, says about Les Fevettes, "I call this my Bordeaux cuvée, because it takes five or six years to open out." Philippe says that increased purity and precision resulted from the conversion to organic viticulture together with the élevage in foudres (since 2006). Depending on quantities, there may be one or two white cuvées (Foudre is the top cuvée), also showing the precise house style.

Domaine Eric Morgat

Clos Ferrand, 49170 Savennières

(33) 02 41 72 22 51

contact@ericmorgat.com

Eric Morgat

www.ericmorgat.com

Savennières

Savennières, L'Enclos

6 ha; 16,000 bottles

Eric Morgat did not go far when he left the family domain, Château de Breuil in the Coteaux du Layon. Crossing the Loire, he established his domain in Savennières. Making a fresh start, vineyards were planted on land that had been uncultivated or long since abandoned. His major vineyard is L'Enclos, 2.9 ha on schist and volcanic rocks in the sector of Beaupréau, planted in several stages since 1995. More recently he has planted another 1.5 ha on the steep slope of La Pierre Bécherelle. (A special tractor is required to work the slope.) He also rents a small plot in Roche aux Moines (so far the wine has been blended into L'Enclos, which remains his sole cuvée from Savennières), and he retained a hectare in the vineyards of Château de Breuil in Beaulieu-sur-Layon when the property was sold in 2006 (this is the Litus cuvée, under the Anjou AOP). Eric's initial vintages were labeled as Domaine de la Monnaie (from the original address of the domain), but since 2002 have been labeled as Domaine éric Morgat. The style has changed a bit, as botrytized grapes are now excluded (although the intention is to go for full maturity) and malolactic fermentation is no longer encouraged. Vinification and élevage are in 400 liter barrels (with up to 20% new wood), and battonage is used, giving a rich modern style. Sometimes there has been a touch of residual sugar, but in principle the wines are dry. There's a definite impression of purity of fruits against that rich background.

Domaine Vincent Ogereau

 44 rue de La Belle Angevine, 49750 Saint Lambert du Lattay

📞 (33) 02 41 78 30 53

@ contact@domaineogereau.com

Vincent Ogereau

🌐 www.domaineogereau.com

Coteaux du Layon

Coteaux du Layon, Harmonie

24 ha; 70,000 bottles

Vincent is the fourth generation at this family domain, established in the 1890s. Vincent took over in 1989—"Being a vigneron always attracted me, as a child I never thought of anything else," he says, although he's also known for playing the tuba. Today his son Emmanuel is helping him (and also plays the tuba). The largest holding (8 ha) is Coteaux du Layon Villages, then there are 2 ha in Savennières, and more in Anjou and Anjou Villages. "We are best known for our Coteaux du Layon. Ogereau may be a small producer but we have the whole range, from rosé to white to red and sweet white, and that is typical of production in the Loire. We have clients who want to buy a range of wines," Emmanuel explains. The mark of the house is to bring out the expression of each variety. Chenin Blanc has a characteristic dry quality in the Savennières, but is given a powerful representation in the Coteaux du Layon, which begins to approach Bonnezeaux in quality. The top wines are the Clos des Bonnes Blanches in Coteaux du Layon St. Lambert, Clos le Grand Beaupréau in Savennières, and Côte de la Houssaye in Anjou-Villages. This last is unusual: a varietal Cabernet Sauvignon. The Ogereaus believe in Cabernet Sauvignon. "We like the extra freshness that comes from Cabernet Sauvignon compared with Cabernet Franc," says Emmanuel. The main difficulty is not so much getting ripeness as avoiding botrytis. In some years the Cabernet Sauvignon goes into the rosé instead of making a red wine.

Château Pierre-Bise

**

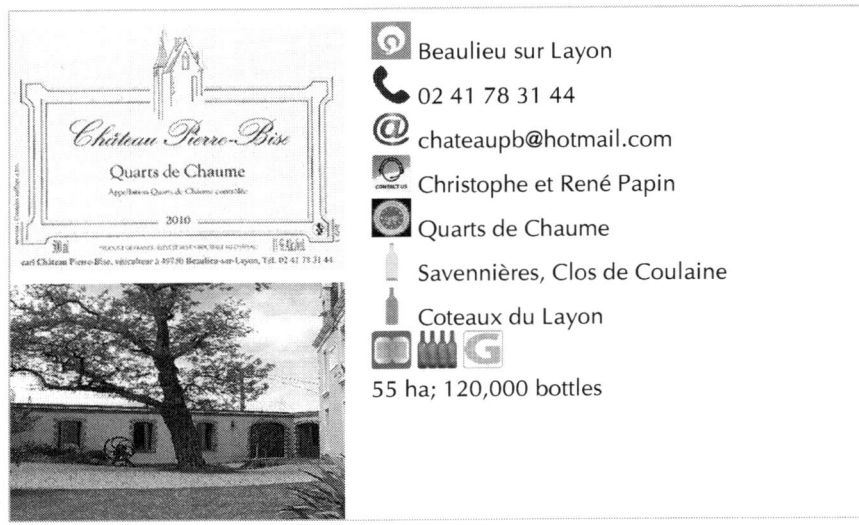

Beaulieu sur Layon

02 41 78 31 44

chateaupb@hotmail.com

Christophe et René Papin

Quarts de Chaume

Savennières, Clos de Coulaine

Coteaux du Layon

55 ha; 120,000 bottles

Château Pierre-Bise is a sixteenth century property on a ridge above the river Layon. The domain started when Pierre Papin purchased the château in 1959 together with 9 ha of vines in Beaulieu-sur-Layon. Claude Papin took over from his father in 1974, and the domain has now grown significantly (partly with vineyards that came with Claude's marriage). It now includes vineyards in three distinct parts of Savennières on the other side of the river. The domain is famous for its sweet Quarts de Chaume and Coteaux du Layon, but the range extends to the (usually dry) three expressions of Savennières; each is considered a definitive representation of its terroir. The vines of Clos de Coulaine are the youngest; at Grand Beaupréau older vines have roots descending into schist or phtanite; and at Roche aux Moines there is more heterogeneity with a partly volcanic terroir. Claude believes that Savennières offers the most complex expression of Chenin: "The variety is a veritable sponge for absorbing terroir," he says. Working the soils here is minimal, as Claude believes that breaking up the surface does more harm than good. Style varies with the vintage, as MLF may or may not occur, and there may or may not be residual sugar (Clos de Coulaine was 'doux' in 2003 but is usually dry). The dry whites have a savory quality, enhanced by the inclusion of some botrytized grapes, which Claude believes enhances the expression of terroir. There are also Anjou reds and rosé.

Domaine Richou

L'**R** d'**A**n**j**°**u**

RDomaine
ı**C H O U**

⊙ Chauvigné, Route de Denée, 49610 Moze-sur-Louet

📞 (33) 02 41 78 72 13

@ domaine.richou@wanadoo.fr

Didier& Damien Richou

🌐 www.domainerichou.fr

Coteaux de l'Aubance

Anjou, Les Rogeries

🚶 ⚗ G 🍇

30 ha; 130,000 bottles

This family domain is divided into 9 parcels, run by third generation Didier Richou together with his brother. The domain had 42 ha, but Didier got rid of 12 ha he did not like. The winery is just off the main road through Mozé-sur-Louet, in the southeastern corner of the Aubance of Anjou. Most of the wines are under the Anjou label, but there are also dry Savennières and sweet Coteaux de l'Aubance. The domain is located in a band of grey schist that runs northwest to southeast across the region, but each of Richou's parcels is different. There are small bands of volcanic terroir, and many small areas with different geologies. Cuvées represent terroirs from schist to volcanic. The wines here are workmanlike, solid representations of their appellations. There is a full range including red, dry and sweet white, rosé, and sparkling. The most interesting wines are those that break out of the mold, such as the Anjou Villages Brissac which is an equal assemblage of Cabernet Franc with Cabernet Sauvignon (from an unusually warm schist terroir that lets the Cabernet Sauvignon ripen), or the L'R Osé, a rosé (from 90% Cabernet Franc and 10% Cabernet Sauvignon) that is not labeled as Cabernet d'Anjou because it is almost dry. Sweet wines depend on the year, with regular production of La Sélection and Les Violettes (passerillé or botrytized depending on conditions), but Les 3 Demoiselles (a late harvest, botrytized Coteaux de l'Aubance from old vines) is produced only in top years.

Château Roche Aux Moines ***

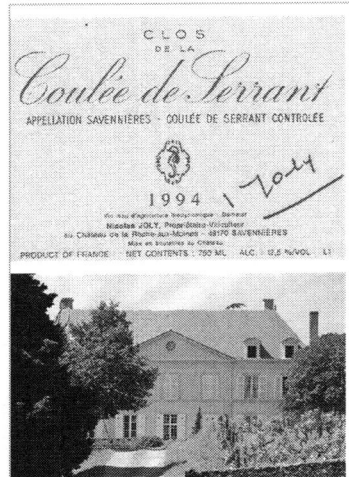

🌐 49170 Savennières

📞 33 (0)2 41 72 22 32

@ coulee-de-serrant@wanadoo.fr

📇 Nicolas Joly

🌐 www.coulee-de-serrant.com

⬤ Savennières

🍾 Coulée de Serrant

15 ha; 32,000 bottles

Nicolas Joly, one of the most famous advocates for biodynamic viticulture, produces three wines at this old domain (supposedly first planted by Cistercian monks). The most famous is Coulée de Serrant (which has its own appellation), but there is also a Savennières, Le Vieux Clos (labeled as Clos Sacré for the United States), from the adjacent vineyard, and Clos de la Bergerie (from Savennières Roche-aux-Moines). "What makes the authenticity of Coulée de Serrant?" Nicolas asks. "Vines have been here for 900 years. The two kinds of terroir—slate and chalk—bring two different types of Chenin. I really feel that Coulée, which has always been a good wine, has improved in the past five years. It has deep roots in the diversity of the geology." All the Joly wines show the same strong style resulting from very late harvest, often so late that there is some botrytis. Sometimes there is a touch of residual sugar. Wines are matured in cuve. "I would be ashamed to put the taste of wood in my wine. It would mean I do not trust my wine enough. We put wine in the cellar in October and we do nothing until we take it out in April," Nicolas says. The wines have been criticized for their high alcohol, often pushing 15%, and I think this is a fair point. The savory intensity and flavor variety are impressive, and the wine has little in common with the pallid offerings of Chenin Blanc often found in the region, but alcohol at 15% can be fatiguing, and it is not unfair to say the wines are more powerful than elegant.

Domaine des Roches Neuves **

56 Boulevard Saint Vincent, 49400 Varrains

(33) 02 41 52 94 02

thierry-germain@wanadoo.fr

Thierry-Germain

www.rochesneuves.com

Saumur-Champigny

Saumur-Champigny, La Marginale

Saumur, L'Insolite

28 ha; 120,000 bottles

Thierry Germain is the six generation of winemakers from Bordeaux but he left Bordeaux in 1991 and bought this old domain in 1996. There was a single tiny building when he started, but this has now been extended into a modern warehouse. He makes 6 red cuvées and 3 whites. Thierry is passionate about terroir and biodynamics; the domain has been biodynamic since 2000. Thierry has a fine reputation for his reds from Saumur-Champigny (which constitute 90% of his production), but I liked his whites just as much, if not more (including a sparkling wine made without dosage). The whites display an unusual precision for Chenin Blanc, with the fine fruits edged by minerality. They need time, not because they are austere, but to let the potential complexity emerge. The reds also point in a mineral direction, and although Thierry's aim is to avoid excess tannin and bring out floral qualities, they can be quite stern and flat when young; here time is needed for the structure to resolve. "I detest Cabernet Franc with tannins that are too powerful. I look for floral notes," Thierry says. "I am against new oak; it always has a tendency to destroy the floral character. I want to express the diversity in the soil." His cuvées come from different terroirs (varying from sandy to calcareous), sometimes from patches of old vines that he has rescued, and he has taken the search for authenticity to the extent of planting a small plot of Cabernet Franc on sandy soil with vines on their own roots.

Clos Rougeard ***

15 rue de l'Eglise, 49400 Chacé

(33) 02 41 52 92 65

gaecfoucault@orange.fr

Jean-Louis Foucault

Saumur-Champigny

Saumur-Champigny, Les Poyeux

Saumur, Le Brézé

10 ha; 22,000 bottles

The unassuming appearance of Clos Rougeard belies its reputation as the best red wine of the Loire. Located in a residential street in Chacé, there is no nameplate or even street number to distinguish the domain. Inside, the house is to one side, and across a courtyard is the entrance to the winery, with a rabbit warren of old caves underneath, carved out of the rock and very cold. The domain has 9.5 ha of Cabernet Franc and 1 ha of Chenin Blanc. The three cuvées of Cabernet Franc are the domain wine (an assemblage of many parcels), Les Poyeux, and Le Bourg: the white comes from Brézé. Les Poyeux is a 3 ha plot of 40-year-old vines with soils varying from clay-silex to clay-calcareous. Le Bourg has 70-year-old vines on clay-calcareous terroir (located behind the house), with 1 ha in two parcels. Usually the reds spend 24 months in barrique, Le Bourg in new barrels, Les Poyeux in older oak. All the cuvées offer an unmistakable impression of pure Cabernet Franc, with a smooth generosity to each wine that, in terms of comparison with Bordeaux, might be regarded as more right bank than left bank. The domain wine is elegant and pure, Les Poyeux is the crystalline essence of Cabernet Franc, and Le Bourg is tighter with higher acidity and tannins, and needs more time. With 20% new oak, Le Brézé offers a wonderfully savory impression of Chenin Blanc. As for methods, "We are very traditional, we are making wine exactly like our parents and grandparents," Nady Foucault says. Vines are maintained by selection massale. There's no chaptalization, no collage, no filtration, no racking (for reds: sometimes there is battonage for whites). The wines are at their best around ten years after the vintage.

Ferme de La Sansonnière

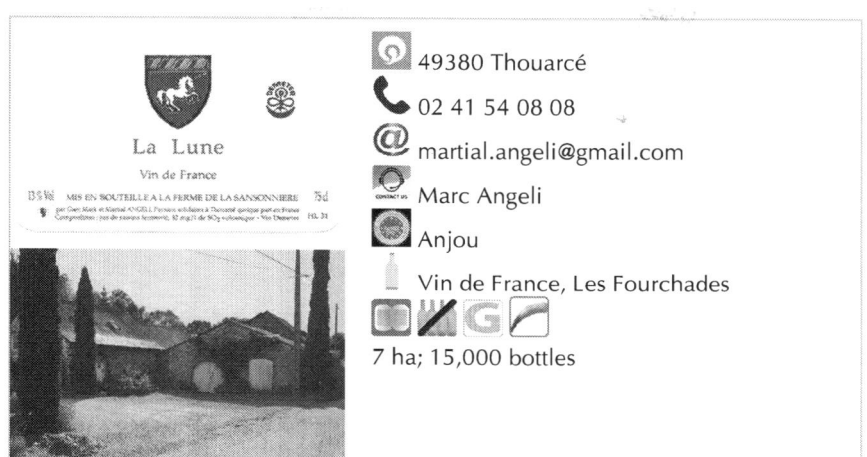

49380 Thouarcé

02 41 54 08 08

martial.angeli@gmail.com

Marc Angeli

Anjou

Vin de France, Les Fourchades

7 ha; 15,000 bottles

Mark Angeli has run this small domain for more than twenty years, and has an influence out of proportion to its size. He is committed to biodynamic viticulture, and together with Virginie Joly organizes an organic fair every July: "The purpose is to say that what is normal is organic," he says. He's had problems with the *agrément* for the AOC, with arguments when he started to make dry white wines (because the general style was sweet at the time) or about the color of his rosés. So now his wines are labeled as Vin de France. The style here is towards flavor. Because winemaking attempts to be as natural as possible, and fermentation is very protracted, the wines are not necessarily completely dry. This can be a problem in maintaining consistency of style. There are three white wines, a sweet rosé, and a red from Grolleau. All the wines except the rosé are matured in old wood. Of the whites, La Lune is a blend from several different plots, in fact covering twelve different terroirs. It's never completely dry and usually ends up with 4-5 g/l residual sugar. Les Fourchades comes from a vineyard just across the road from the winery. Les Blanderies Vieilles Vignes comes from 76-year-old vines and is the most savory of the whites. Mark sums up his approach by saying, "I'm very annoyed when people say that a winegrower is an artist—there is no artistry in this job. We have to take decisions that are very important, we are artisans but not artists. Most important is when to harvest."

Château Soucherie

La Soucherie, 49750 Beaulieu-sur-Layon

(33) 02 41 78 31 18

contact@domaine-de-la-soucherie.com

Maxime Séjourné

www.domaine-de-la-soucherie.fr

Coteaux du Layon

Coteaux du Layon, Chaume

28 ha; 100,000 bottles

Château Soucherie was originally a farm owned by the Duke of Brissac, and the Château was built as a leisure house. Sold to the Tijou family between the wars, it was bought by its present owners in 2007, who put in place a new, young team. The property is on a high point, running down to the river, with 22 ha of the vineyards immediately around. All the vineyards are on schist, although the type of schist varies, facing south, and protected from the north wind. There is a wide range of wines. Most plantings are Chenin Blanc, for the Coteaux du Layon and Anjou Blanc. The top wines come from 4 ha in Chaume and 2 ha in Savennières (the Clos des Perrières). There is no MLF for the whites. Cabernet Franc is grown on the slopes for the Anjou reds, and there is also some Grolleau. The house style is quite delicate and concerned to preserve freshness, which is why they want no botrytis in the dry white wines. (Botrytis develops rapidly here because the vineyards are close to the river. Handpicking is essential to exclude botrytized grapes from the dry whites.) "For us the schist is really tremendous for the dry and sweet white wines, but for Cabernet Franc schist is not an easy expression, the finish is always a little tannic, we are looking for fruit to balance the tannins in Anjou Rouge, and for more structure and a velvety quality for the Cru; but always with the freshness that for us is typical of the Loire valley," says marketing manager Florence de Barmon.

Château de Villeneuve

Château de Villeneuve
2009
SAUMUR CHAMPIGNY

Chevallier Père & Fils, 49400 Souzay Champigny

(33) 02 41 51 14 04

jp-chevallier@chateau-de-villeneuve.com

Jean-Pierre Chevallier

www.chateau-de-villeneuve.com

Saumur

Saumur-Champigny, Le Grand Clos

25 ha; 140,000 bottles

The magnificent eighteenth century château stands on a plateau above the Loire, looking over the cliff to the river beyond. Vineyards run back from the château, which was purchased in 1969 by Jean-Pierre Chevallier's parents. Jean-Pierre took over in 1982, and has moved into organic viticulture, with the introduction of cover crops to control fertility. "But sometimes the cover crops can impede maturity of the grapes," he says. As well as four cuvées of Saumur-Champigny, there are two white Saumurs. Cabernet Franc has cold soak of 5-6 days, and remains in wooden tronconique cuves for a month at temperatures below 23 degrees; élevage is in 500 liter casks varying from new to 3 years old. Sulfur levels are kept low. Besides the château bottling, there are cuvées from two lieu-dits, Le Clos immediately around the château and the 1.5 ha Clos de la Bienboire, and also a Vieilles Vignes assemblage from three parcels. The old vines are used for selection massale to replant the other vineyards. The style here is quite solid: these are well made wines in which you see the characteristics of the Chenin Blanc and Cabernet Franc varieties in Saumur and Saumur-Champigny. The cuvées are not quite as distinctive as I would have liked. "You can keep the cuvées of Saumur-Champigny for 15 or 20 years, it's not a problem, but generally we drink immediately after bottling when they still have fermentation and other volatile aromas, or we wait three or four years," says Jean-Pierre.

Touraine

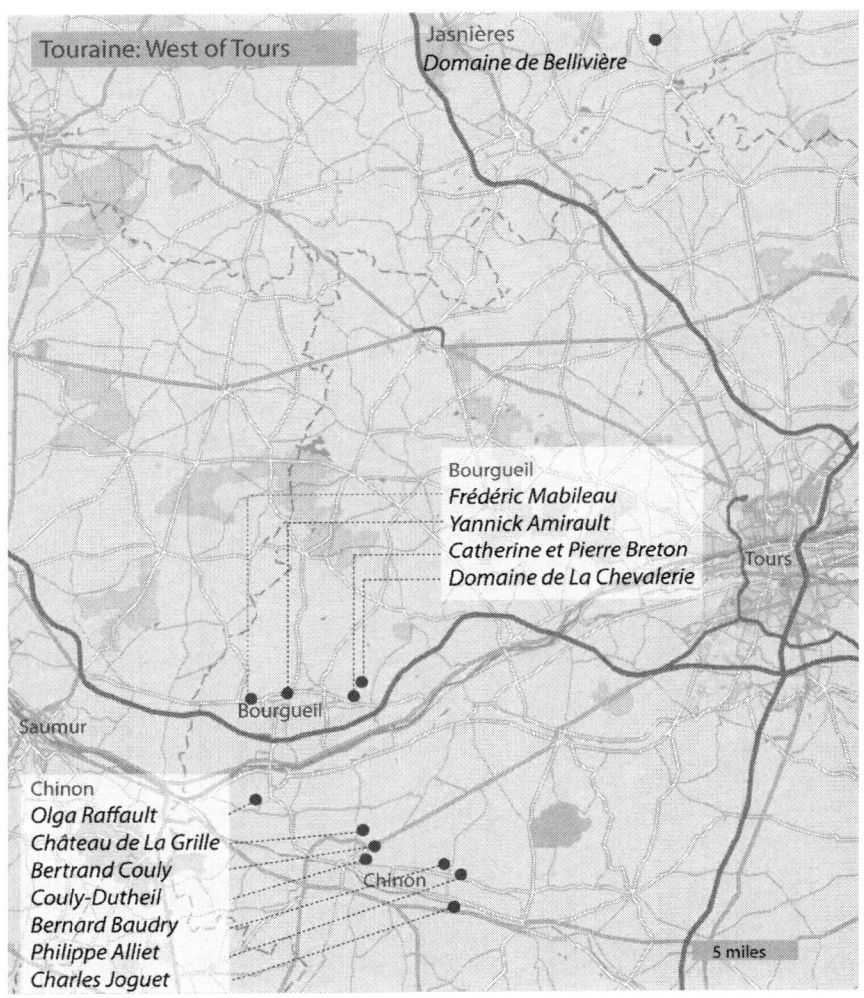

Touraine: West of Tours

Jasnières
Domaine de Bellivière

Bourgueil
Frédéric Mabileau
Yannick Amirault
Catherine et Pierre Breton
Domaine de La Chevalerie

Tours

Bourgueil

Saumur

Chinon
Olga Raffault
Château de La Grille
Bertrand Couly
Couly-Dutheil
Bernard Baudry
Philippe Alliet
Charles Joguet

Chinon

5 miles

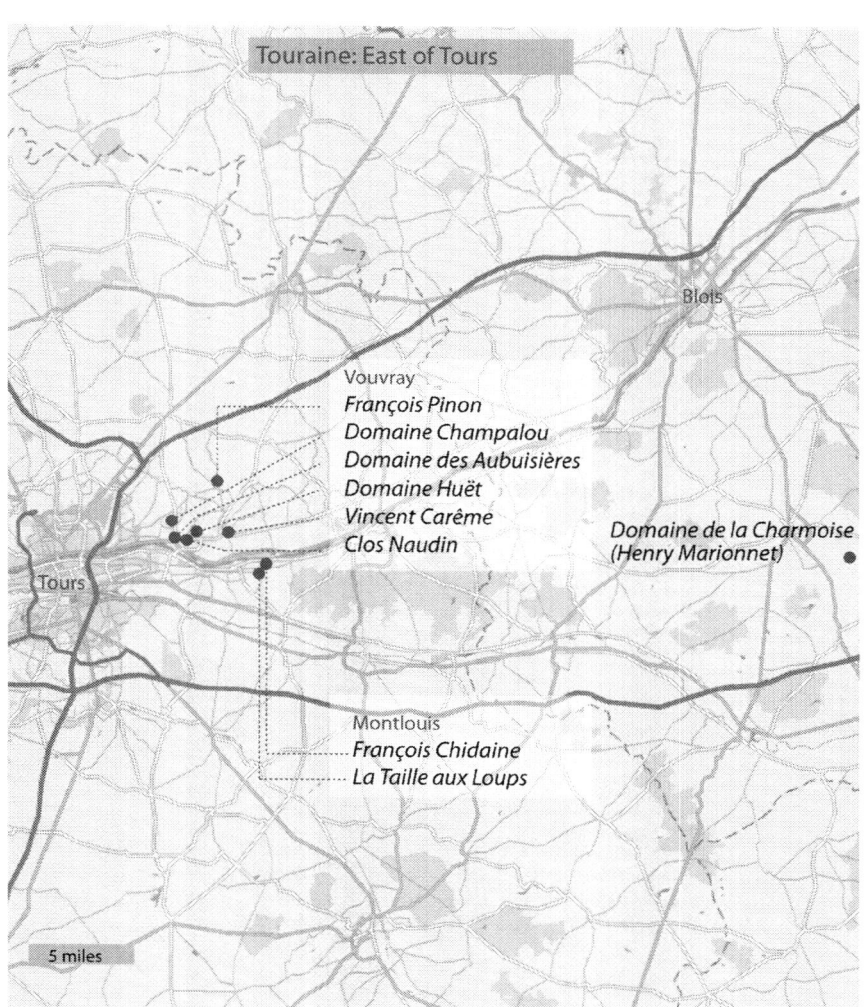

Touraine: East of Tours

Blois

Tours

Vouvray
François Pinon
Domaine Champalou
Domaine des Aubuisières
Domaine Huët
Vincent Carême
Clos Naudin

Domaine de la Charmoise
(Henry Marionnet)

Montlouis
François Chidaine
La Taille aux Loups

5 miles

Domaine Philippe Alliet

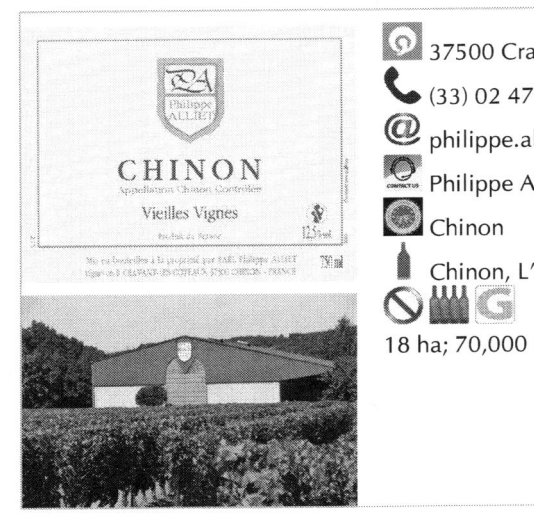

CHINON
Appellation Chinon Contrôlée

Vieilles Vignes

🎯 37500 Cravant Les Côteaux

📞 (33) 02 47 93 17 62

@ philippe.alliet@wanadoo.fr

Philippe Alliet

Chinon

Chinon, L'Huisserie

18 ha; 70,000 bottles

"My father is passionate for Bordeaux," says Pierre Alliet, who joined his father in 2003. Philippe created the domain in the eighties with 4 ha which came from his great grandfather. The winery is a practical building on the main road out of Chinon to the east. The domain has expanded to offer four cuvées, all from Chinon. The model is traditional, with duration of aging, and oak exposure, increasing as the wines become more complex, but the reputation of the domain for always using very high proportions of new oak is exaggerated. Classique comes from 15-year-old vines on sandy-gravel soils and is vinified in cement, with 18 months aging. "We don't like stainless steel, it gives too much reduction," says Pierre. L'Huisserie comes from the most recently acquired vineyard, planted in 2001 on siliceous soils. The wine spends 6 months in cement, 7 months in wooden fûts, and then a final 6 months in cement. Philippe's most famous holding is the Coteaux de Noiré, a steep south-facing slope with very calcareous terroir that he planted in 1996. This is in the best known part of the appellation, between Chinon itself (within sight of the Château) and Cravant-les-Côteaux. It spends 4 months in cement, 12 months in new barriques (where malolactic fermentation takes place), and then a final 6 months in cement. In response to criticism that new oak does not express the character of Chinon, Philippe's response is to ask, "What is a typical Chinon? No one knows. In any case, not dilute wine with a nose of green pepper." Classique is straightforward, L'Huisserie offers a more mineral impression, and Coteaux de Noiré offers the most finesse and precision. The top wines seem to peak about 8 years after the vintage.

Domaine Yannick Amirault

5 Pavillon du Grand Clos, 37140 Bourgueil

(33) 02 47 97 78 07

info@yannickamirault.fr

Yannick Amirault

www.yannickamirault.fr

Bourgueil

St. Nicolas de Bourgueil, Les Malgagnes

19 ha; 90,000 bottles

The domain is located in an unassuming house opposite the vineyard, but at the rear is a practical, modern winery. The domain started in 1936; since Yannick took over in 1989 he has more or less doubled the size. "But now it is going to stop," he says. There are 25 separate parcels, with 13 ha in Bourgueil and 7 ha in St. Nicolas de Bourgueil. "The particularity of the domain is that all the wines are vinified in wood, varying from barriques to large casks," Yannick says. "The potential for aging is the most important thing." The style is somewhat stern, showing quite strong tannins, the fruits tend to be earthy, and there is a stony sense to the finish. This theme runs through all the wines, from the lightest entry level to those that Yannick regards as his Crus. The style is towards vins de garde, but I sometimes worry whether the fruits are generous enough to support really long aging. The entry level wine, La Coudraye, which comes from sandy soil around the winery, is the lightest; Les Malgagnes comes from calcareous terroir and has more generosity; Les Quartiers comes from 60-year old vines on white limestone, and Le Grand Clos comes from 50-year old vines on a mix of soils including silex. There is increasing weight going up the hierarchy. In addition to the reds, there is also a rosé. "Usually rosés have some residual sugar but I want to make a dry rosé," says Yannick. "It is my white wine." The wines represent a definite philosophy. "There is a place for wines with strong personality."

Domaine des Aubuisières

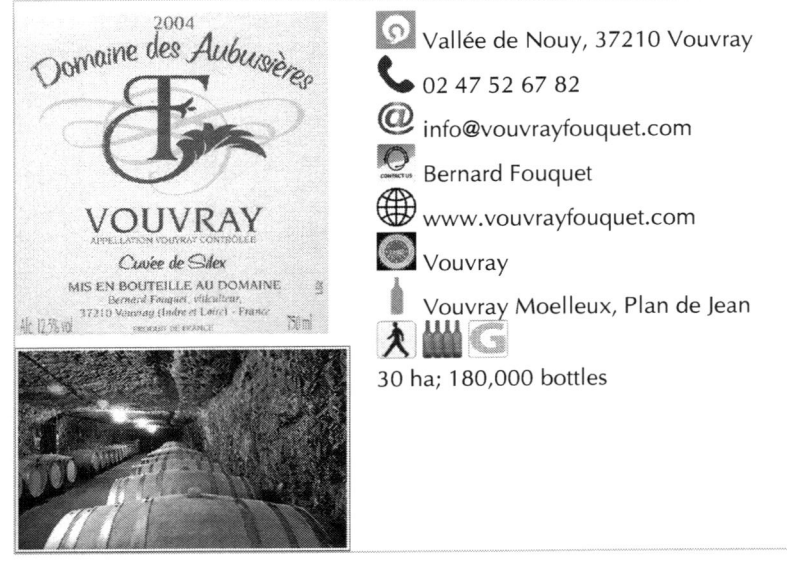

Vallée de Nouy, 37210 Vouvray

02 47 52 67 82

info@vouvrayfouquet.com

Bernard Fouquet

www.vouvrayfouquet.com

Vouvray

Vouvray Moelleux, Plan de Jean

30 ha; 180,000 bottles

The winery occupies a warehouse in a back street of Vouvray—access was blocked by a huge truck loading wine for Majestic in England when I visited—but inside at the back is a neat tasting room seemingly carved out of the rock face. "I'm the first generation," says Bernard Fouquet when asked about the history of the domain. He started in 1982 with 5 ha; today 50% of the vineyards are on clay-calcareous soils and 50% are on clay-silex soils. "I have different cuvées, of course, that reflect the terroirs," he says. Four come from the calcareous terroirs (Le Marigny, Le Bouchet, Le Plan de Jean, Le Clos de L'Auberdière), and three from silex (Les Girardières, Les Perruches, Les Chairs Salées). Some of the dry wines and the demi-sec are matured in cuve, but the sweeter wines are matured in wood. "You do not see the minerality if you vinify in cuve, you need to use wood; the cuve emphasizes aromatics," Bernard explains. He believes the wines require time to show complexity—the sweeter the wine, the longer it takes to show its character—and is concerned that most are drunk too early. "People drink the wines far too young. I am sure that all the 2009 and 2010, I have sold have already been consumed. It is a great pity, but people won't wait any more." There is an extensive range here, from dry through demi-sec to liquoreux, all Vouvray AOP. The style of the domain shows best at the moelleux level, with the maturation in wood bringing an attractive smokiness to the finish.

Domaine Bernard Baudry

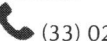 13 Coteaux de Sonnay, 37500 Cravant Les Côteaux

📞 (33) 02 47 93 15 79

@ bernard-baudry@chinon.com

 Mathieu Baudry

 www.chinon.com/vignoble/bernard-baudry

 Chinon

🍾 Chinon, La Croix Boisée

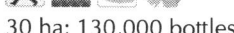

30 ha; 130,000 bottles

The domain was created in 1975, but there was a long prior history of winegrowing in the family. Mathieu Baudry joined his father in 2000. On the main road just outside Cravant Les Côteaux, a courtyard leads to an old house, but a modern winery has been built in a warehouse behind. The estate is 98% Cabernet Franc and 2% Chenin Blanc. Vineyards are dispersed around the valley, coteaux, and plateau; most are in Cravant but some are in Chinon. There are five red cuvées and two white, each representing a different terroir from estate vineyards. "We work in the spirit of Burgundy, with the same cépage but different terroirs. It is not an obligation of the appellation, it's a personal choice," says Mathieu. "Our aim is to get transparency of terroir in the wine." There is a pretty good correlation between terroir and wine style here, with the sandy soils of the domain Chinon producing light fresh wine, a more gravelly texture emerging from the pebbly soil of Les Grezeaux, a somewhat more chalky impression appearing as you move into the limestone of Clos Guillot, and then full force fruits showing as the soil becomes clay-limestone at La Croix Boisée. The reds become steadily rounder and riper as the proportion of limestone increases. Within Clos Guillot there is a small patch of vines planted on their own roots. La Croix Boisée produces two wines, red and white, with the white coming from the most calcareous terroir.

Domaine de Bellivière

Bellivière, 72340 L'homme

(33) 02 43 44 59 97

info@belliviere.com

Eric & Christine Nicolas

www.belliviere.com

Jasnières

Jasnières, Calligramme

15 ha; 43,000 bottles

Jasnières is decidedly off the beaten track, well to the north of the Loire. But here Eric Nicolas has made a name not only for his Jasnières (Chenin Blanc) but also for his cuvées from Pineau d'Aunis, an old red variety of the Loire that is now quite rare (although it remains the principle red variety for Coteaux du Loir. The domain started in 1995 with 3.5 ha in Coteaux du Loir. Today the vineyards are divided between Jasnières and Coteaux du Loir, mostly planted with Chenin Blanc. Vineyards are perpetuated by selection massale, and there are experiments in planting vines at very high density. White wines are vinified and matured in 1- to 3-year-old barrels; there is no MLF or battonage. Rosés are vinified in old barrels, and reds are vinified in open top vats followed by maturation in barrique (with very little new wood). The 4 ha of Pineau make two Coteaux du Loir red wines: the Rouge-Gorge cuvée comes from young vines; l'Hommage à Louis Derré comes from hundred-year-old vines. Depending on the vintage, there may also be some rosé (which may include a little Grolleau), labeled as Vin de France, in varying styles of sweetness. The white wines include both dry and sweet styles from both Jasnières and Coteaux du Loir. The Jasnières include Les Rosiers (from young vines), Calligramme (from old vines)—these may vary from dry to off-dry styles depending on the vintage—and the sweet wines, Discours de Tuf and Elixir de Tuf from selections of botrytized grapes.

Domaine Catherine et Pierre Breton

37420 Beaumont-en-Véron

(33) 02 47 97 30 41

domainebreton@yahoo.fr

Pierre Breton

www.domainebreton.net

Chinon

Bourgueil, Les Galichets

11 ha; 80,000 bottles

The first time I visited the Bretons, I went to a charming old property in the middle of the vineyards. The house and old cave are still used for visits by tourists (and for élevage) but the main facility for fermentation and handling moved to a warehouse on an industrial estate in 2012. It's not glamorous, but it's rather more practical. "Moving wasn't to expand, it was just to have more room to work. We were surprised to realize that we had managed to fit everything in before," Catherine says. There's a wide range of wines, with an emphasis on natural production. Sulfur use is minimized, and sulfur is not used before bottling. There is one completely sulfur-free wine (d'Ivresse) where sulfite is not used even on the grapes. The house style is for a certain finesse (the entry-level wines are of course simpler), but after that there is real refinement—and at moderate alcohol. Why don't you have a problem with increasing alcohol, I asked? "But we do. In 1998 we were getting 10.5-11% alcohol—we never chaptalized but chaptalization was common in the Loire. We have probably gained 1% alcohol. Alcohol hit 13% only in 2003." Production is about two thirds Bourgueil to a third Chinon. There is also some Vouvray and IGP. The most interesting reds come from Bourgueil, where there is a fascinating opportunity to compare the conventional bottling from Les Galichets with a small plot of Franc de Pied (vines on their own roots), which is the epitome of refinement.

Vincent Carême

Domaine
Vincent Carême

VOUVRAY TENDRE

Vernou-sur-Brenne, 37210

(33) 02 47 52 71 28

@ vincentcareme@vinibegood.com

Vincent Carême

vin@vincentcareme.fr

Vouvray

Vouvray Sec, Peu Morier

14 ha; 45,000 bottles

Vincent Carême took over the vines of his parents and established this domain in 1999 after working in Muscadet, Alsace, and South Africa to gain experience. He's now considered to be one of the leading vignerons of the new generation. There is a small cellar in a back street of Vernou (well, they are all back streets in Vernou). Vineyards are all on the première côte in Vouvray, the first slope that runs up from the town, except for a tiny parcel that is used for production of Vin de France. The vineyards were converted to organic between 2007 and 2010. There are two sparkling wines and six still wines (including moelleux and liquoreux cuvées that are made only in some years). The Brut is made by méthode traditionelle, while a second sparkling wine is made by méthode ancestrale. The Sec and Tendre cuvées come from the same vineyard; Tendre is a demi-sec with 20 g/l of residual sugar. Two cuvées (usually dry) come from single parcels: Peu Monier comes from clay-silex, and Le Clos from pure limestone (usually it is sec but in 2008 it made a demi-sec). Everything here is always matured in barriques of old oak. Any residual sugar is a consequence of fermentation stopping naturally. There is sometimes partial malolactic fermentation. The house style tends to be quite powerful and fruity with a texture on the palate coming from the extended maturation in wood. There is good flavor concentration and the impression of richness is accentuated by the relatively high alcohol.

Domaine Champalou

Le Portail, 7 rue Grand Ormeau, 37210 Vouvray

(33) 02 47 52 64 49

champalou@wanadoo.fr

Catherine, Céline & Didier Champalou

www.champalou.com

Vouvray

Vouvray, Les Fondraux

20 ha; 120,000 bottles

The domain was created in 1995 by Catherine and Didier Champalou. Catherine is the eleventh generation of a winemaking family, but did not inherit the familial domain because she was a girl. But she is attached to her roots. Didier isn't from the region, but after going to oenology school decided to settle on Vouvray because he liked the idea of being able to produce a range of wines from one cépage. The cave is built into the hillside, with an old section at the back, but is mostly a modern concrete facility built in 2004. From 1.8 ha initially, the domain has grown to have vineyards in 47 separate parcels in 3 of the 8 communes of Vouvray. "At the start it was easy to buy vineyards because no one wanted them. An old vigneron would say, 'I'm retiring,' and would be glad to hand his vines on," Catherine recollects. Every parcel is vinified separately. There is assemblage for 4-6 different cuvées (moelleux and liquoreux are not made every year). At lower sweetness levels, neither sec nor demi-sec is indicated on the label. "People know that Fondraux is our demi-sec," Catherine says. The style of the wines is distinctly modern, although it goes in two directions. The dry whites either show the freshness of stainless steel vinification or they go to the extreme of barrel fermentation in new barriques, with quite overwhelming oak in the Le Portail cuvée. Why did you create this, I asked? "Because of you the journalists. This was basically to make a more international wine."

Domaine de La Charmoise ★★

CEPAGE ROMORANTIN

Provignage

2011

Vigne pré-phylloxérique
Mis en bouteille au domaine de la Charmoise
Henry et Jean-Sébastien Marionnet
Vignerons à Soings (Loir-et-Cher) France
PRODUCE OF FRANCE   750 ml

La Charmoise, 41230 Soings-en-Sologne

(33) 02 54 98 70 73

henry@henry-marionnet.com

Henry & Jean-Sébastien Marionnet

www.henry-marionnet.com

Touraine

Touraine, Sauvignon Blanc Le Vinifera

60 ha; 400,000 bottles

"We'll compare the normal cuvée—well, there is nothing normal here—with the ungrafted vines," Henry says, as we start our tasting at Domaine de la Charmoise. Henry's father started the domain before the first world war, but he had 20 ha of hybrids. Henry built it up to its present level, mostly with Gamay and Sauvignon Blanc, but with an interest in reviving the original wines of the area, in this case meaning cultivating some old varieties, planting vines on their own roots, and making wine without adding sulfur. Today his son Jean-Sébastien is the winemaker, but Henry is still very much in evidence. The estate is lies on a high point between the Loire and Cher rivers, at the eastern edge of Touraine, and has the classic "perruches" soil of clay, flint and gravel. Two thirds of plantings are black varieties (90% Gamay), and one third is white (almost all Sauvignon Blanc). The unique feature of the domain is a focus on ungrafted vines, which form the basis for the Vinifera cuvées, including Chenin Blanc, Sauvignon Blanc, Gamay, and Malbec. These come from 6 ha of vineyards planted relatively recently, but the Provignage cuvée comes from a small plot of pre-phylloxera vines of Romorantin. "These are the oldest vines in France," Jean-Sébastien says, as he shows off the vineyard. They were part of a 4 ha vineyard that Henry Marionnet bought in 1998, but under the previous owner the grapes were just included in the mix sold to the cooperative. Another throwback is the Cépages Oubliés, which comes from an old clone of Gamay, the Gamay de Bouze, which has colored juice, and was relatively common until it was banned by INAO. The Première Vendange cuvée is bottled without sulfur. Renaissance is a two-fer, coming from ungrafted vines and having no sulfur. Jean-Sébastien first made it in

2014. Vinified in stainless steel in completely modern cellars (there is no oak here), the style focuses on purity of fruit—"The ideal is to make wine without interference," Jean-Sébastien says. There is usually some carbonic maceration for the Gamay. With each variety, the normal cuvée is very good—the Gamay is often compared favorably with Beaujolais and the Sauvignon with Sancerre—but Vinifera shows an extra level of purity. When you taste the Gamay, you think, this is very good, it puts most Beaujolais to shame, then when you taste Première Vendange, you think, this goes a step further, and then Renaissance pushes that back. Each wine successively becomes more subtle and complex. "This is a pure wine, no sulfur, no rootstock," Henry says when we reach Renaissance. Gamay is the heart of the domain: "here you drink Gamay and you eat Gamay," Henry comments as we finish lunch at the domain with a fruit tart made from Gamay, with a sauce made from Gamay de Bouze. The top wine among the regular cuvées is the M de Marionnet, a Sauvignon Blanc.

Domaine de La Chevalerie

DOMAINE DE LA
CHEVALERIE
Stéphanie, Emmanuel & Pierre CASLOT
BOURGUEIL

Chevalerie
2001

7 rue du Peu Muleau, 37140 Restigné

(33) 02 47 97 37 18

@ chevalerie@caslot.fr

Stephanie Caslot

www.domainedelachevalerie.fr

Bourgueil

Bourgueil, Busardières

38 ha; 120,000 bottles

The Caslot family founded this domain in 1640, and today it is run by the fourteenth generation, Stéphanie (the winemaker) and Emmanuel (vineyard manager). The house is above one of Touraine's largest cellars, excavated during the eleventh and thirteenth centuries to provide stone to construct the village of Restigné; converted to wine cellars in the eighteenth century, the caves actually cover around a hectare. It's one of the most picturesque wine sites of the region, but the wines are completely serious. Extending all around the house, 24 ha of vineyards are divided into six blocks with soils varying from sandy to clay. Grapes from another area to the north are sold off to negociants. The wines are exclusively Cabernet Franc under the Bourgueil AOP. The focus is on what the Caslots call Cuvées Parcellaires, coming from single vineyards. House style tends to freshness with almost racy acidity on the palate, and manages to convey a sense of the typicity of Cabernet Franc through the entire range. The lightest cuvées are matured in cuve: Diptique comes from several small parcels in the plain around the village, while Peu Muleau comes from the top of the plateau from sandy terroir. All the other cuvees are matured in tonneaux. Coming from terroir that's a mix of sand and clay, Galichets tends to be the most fruity, while Chevalerie comes from 70-year-old vines around the winery, just above Galichets, and has longer élevage. Busardières comes from 50-year-old vines on calcareous terroir and is the most structured, while Grand Mont comes from a cooler spot in the neighboring village of Benais and is just a touch denser. There's very little new oak; a small amount (about 5%) is used only for Grand Mont. "We are looking for finesse, new oak does not really suit our style," Stéphanie says. The top cuvées age well for several years. Occasionally there are special cuvées, usually to mark a great vintage.

François Chidaine

○ 30 quai Albert Baillet, 37270 Montlouis-sur-Loire

☎ (33) 02 47 45 19 14

@ lacaveinsolite@hotmail.com

👤 François Chidaine

🌐 www.francois-chidaine.com

◉ Montlouis

🍾 Montlouis, Les Bournais

🚶 ⛪ G ⟋

37 ha; 150,000 bottles

François Chidaine is somewhat of a mover and shaker in Montlouis, where he has a wine shop (La Cave Insolite) in the main street that offers tastings of his wines and an excellent selection of bottles from the region and elsewhere. François founded the domain 25 years ago with 3 ha, and he also owns a domain in Spain (his wife is Spanish). Today the domain consists of many small parcels, totaling 10 ha in Vouvray, 20 ha in Montlouis, and 7 ha in Touraine. There is a complete range from dry to fully sweet still wines and also sparkling wines. The wines offer a rare opportunity to compare those of Montlouis and Vouvray directly. The dry wines are not necessarily completely dry, and Chidaine does not mark sec or demi-sec on the label as the objective is to look for balance in which the sugar is not intended to be a noticeable feature. The view here is that anything up to 6-7 g/l residual sugar is effectively dry: "There is always a roundness," they say at the domain. The best dry white comes from Le Bournais in Montlouis, where there is a small patch of ungrafted vines whose lower yield gives a wine with distinctly more intensity and character (and a price to match). There is one moelleux each from Vouvray and Montlouis, and a liquoreux is made in exceptional vintages. The difference in terroirs shows most clearly at the moelleux level, where the Vouvray has a similar flavor spectrum but distinctly more intensity than the Montlouis.

Pierre et Bertrand Couly

PIERRE & BERTRAND COULY

CHINON
Appellation d'Origine Contrôlée

La Haute Olive

2012

4, rue de Saint-Louans, 37500 Chinon

02 47 93 43 97

contact@pb-couly.com

Bertrand Couly

www.pb-couly.com

Chinon

Chinon, St. Louans Le Parc

20 ha; 100,000 bottles

Bertrand has been making wine since 1985, but started this domain with his father in 2007 after a disagreement caused them to leave the old family domain, Couly-Dutheil. The heart of the new domain is vineyards from Bertrand's maternal ancestors, which go back to the fifteenth century, but the winery is new. "St. Louans is a very old village, and is not very convenient for modern life, so we decided to build a new winery, and as it's not in a place with old buildings, we decided to use modern architecture," says Bertrand. Dominating a major intersection out of town, the tasting room is a striking circular building, adjacent to the winery which is a large construction built into the hillside, with a living roof on which a vineyard has been planted. (Bertrand has been allowed by the town to plant vines on the rotary at the intersection, but not to make wine from them.) "It's a modern winery but our wines are in the tradition of the appellation," Bertrand says. "As we have only one variety—Cabernet Franc—each wine is a different story because of the terroir. To keep the potential of each terroir, there's aging only in stainless steel, there is no use of barriques." Cuvées are distinguished by different sources. A saignée from all lots is used to make a rosé, then the Classic cuvée comes from sandy soil, La Haute Olive comes from a south-facing vineyard near the winery where the terroir is limestone and tufa (from which the castle at Chinon was built), St. Louans Le Parc comes from vines around the family house on sandy soil above limestone, which gives smaller berries and more concentration, and V de Pierre and Bertrand comes from clay and limestone soil to the west of Chinon. Cabernet Franc shows clearly through the whole range: Classic is the entry-level—"Light fruits, nice summer wine," says Bertrand; La Haute Olive is smooth and supple, and still on the light side; St. Louans Le Parc is more structured but still quite delicate; and V de Pierre and Bertrand is the most structured and is held back for later release—the 2011 was the current release in 2016. The general house style goes for elegance rather than extraction to showcase the aromatic qualities of Cabernet Franc.

Maison Couly-Dutheil **

🔘 Couly-Dutheil, 12, rue Diderot, 37500 Chinon

📞 (33) 02 47 97 20 20

@ info@coulydutheil-chinon.com

👤 Arnaud Couly-Dutheil

🌐 www.coulydutheil-chinon.com

🍇 Chinon

🍾 Chinon, Clos de l'Echo

94 ha; 500,000 bottles

Founded in the 1920s after René Couly married Madelaine Dutheil, Couly-Dutheil became one of the largest producers in Chinon under René, who passed the domain to his sons Jacques and Pierre. Long recognized as the top red wine producer in Chinon, Couly-Dutheil went through a sticky patch in the late nineties, after which a disagreement in the 2000s between the brothers led to a split. Jacques (who died in 2016) continued to run the domain together with his son Arnaud. Pierre left to found a new domain with his son Bertrand. Located in the center of Chinon, Couly-Dutheil has a modern winery on multiple storeys to allow gravity operation; underneath are miles of old caves. There are extensive vineyard holdings (almost all Cabernet Franc in Chinon), but grapes are also purchased from other growers to round out the line. Arnaud, who started in 2000 after experience in the United States, introduced a policy of picking later to increase ripeness, and in 2003 stopped using barriques in favor of stainless steel. The entry level wine, Les Gravières, comes from gravel terroir near the Vienne river. "The object here is to have fruits that are easy to drink," said Jacques Couly. Baronnie Madeleine, from the middle of the range offers a softer impression. The top wines come from two monopoles, Clos de l'Olive (a 5 ha *clos* purchased in 1951); the south-facing slope still has some hundred-year-old vines. Clos de l'Echo, the only vineyard actually in the town of Chinon, was purchased in 1925 when production began, and remains the heart of the domain. Somewhat larger, around 13 ha, it has a variety of exposures, ranging from a flat plateau, farthest from the town, to quite a steep slope running down to the walls of the castle at the bottom.

Given the variety of terroirs, "The wine is an assemblage in Bordeaux style," said Jacques Couly. Pure fruits meld into mineral and earthy impressions with a touch of tobacco: the epitome of Cabernet Franc, and you would swear that barrique aging had been used to achieve this complexity of texture. Crescendo is a second wine from Clos de l'Echo that continues to be matured in (new) barriques. It's very good, an example of fully ripe Cabernet Franc, but for me the oak obscures the typicity of the variety.

Château de La Grille

37500 Chinon

(33) 02 47 93 01 95

chateaudelagrille@wanadoo.fr

Jean-Martin Dutour

www.chateaudelagrille.com

Chinon

Chinon, Château de la Grille

27 ha; 150,000 bottles

Château la Grille was owned by the Gosset family (of Gosset Champagne) until it was sold in 2009 to Jean-Martin Dutour, who also owns three other properties: Domaine de la Perrière, Domaine de Roncé, and Château de St. Louand. The total of 150 ha makes Jean-Martin the largest owner of vineyards in Chinon. The properties are used more or less as an ascending hierarchy (although with a little overlap between the special cuvée of one Château and the regular cuvée of the next Château). Altogether there are 10 principal cuvées. Domaine de la Perrière (on recent alluvial soils in the valley) is directed towards easy drinking wines; Domaine de Roncé (on an ancient terrace) is more tense and tannic; Château de la Grille (coming from relatively homogeneous limestone and clay) is a vin de garde in the middle of the range (50% matured in barriques and 50% in cuve); and Château de St Louand (calcareous terroir on the plateau) is matured entirely in new barriques. It's really only when you get to Château de la Grille that you see the typicity of Cabernet Franc breaking out. This is a mainstream Chinon, as opposed to the Château de Saint Louand which is distinctly in an international style. At Château de la Grille, half of the 27 ha surround the château; the other half is on a slope across the nearby autoroute, planted almost entirely in Cabernet Franc. There's been a large investment here, with a new gravity-feed winery underground, and a modern tasting room.

Domaine Huët

Le Haut Lieu, 37210 Vouvray

(33) 02 47 52 78 87

contact@huet-echansonne.com

Jean Bernard Berthomé

www.huet-echansonne.com

Vouvray

Vouvray Moelleux, Le Mont

30 ha; 100,000 bottles

Founded in 1928 by Victor Huët with his son Gaston, this is the most famous domain in Vouvray. Gaston's son-in-law Noël Pinguet became the third winemaker. With Gaston in ill-health, the domain was sold to the Hwang family, who are interested in sweet wines and also have a domain in Tokaji. Noël Pinguet retired in 2012 amid reports of disagreements about style and quality. Hugo Hwang and his sister Sarah now run the property. "The goal of the domain is to make sweet wine, that is the tradition," says Hugo, "but it changes from year to year." The domain has three vineyards. The 5 ha of Le Haut Lieu were the origin of the estate; Clos du Bourg (one of the oldest vineyards in the region) was added in 1953; and Le Mont was added in 1957. All the vineyards are on the slope of the Première Côte running up from the river. There is a range of wines, from dry to fully sweet, from each vineyard; the usual balance is about 40% dry to 60% in various sweet styles (demi-sec, moelleux, and moelleux Première Trie). The sweet wines are the glory of the domain, but terroir shows through all: the moelleux most clearly typify the classic acid-sweet balance of Vouvray. These are very fine wines, which certainly can stand up to dessert wines produced anywhere in the world by the point 1er Trie moelleux is reached. Cuvée Constance is a selection of the most botrytized berries, made only occasionally. About 20% of production goes into méthode traditionelle and pétillant sparkling wines.

Domaine Charles Joguet

Les Varennes du Grand Clos
CHINON

CHARLES JOGUET

La Dioterie, 37220 Sazilly

(33) 02 47 58 55 53

joguet@charlesjoguet.com

Alain Delaunay

www.charlesjoguet.com

Chinon

Chinon, Clos du Chêne Vert

38 ha; 150,000 bottles

The winery was originally a farm, before Charles Joguet converted it exclusively to viticulture when he came back to Sazilly from art studies in Paris in 1959. Following the model of Burgundy, he decided to see what effect terroir would have in Chinon, and introduced cuvées from different vineyards. Charles retired in 1997, and since then the domain has been owned by the Genet family. "He was quite an innovator, some things worked, some didn't," recalls current winemaker Kevin Fontaine. Joguet had the first stainless steel tanks in the Loire: today they are the standard. The focus remains on cuvées from different terroirs, although there have been some changes in the vineyard holdings. The style here tends to freshness, with increasing fruit density and structure going up the scale; the wines are never aggressive or heavy. Ascending the hierarchy of the red cuvées, Cuvée Terroir (from sandy soils), Les Petites Roches (an assemblage from several parcels), and Cuvée de la Cure (from clay and gravel terroir around the church) are relatively straightforward. The other terroirs are clay and limestone. There's a step up with Les Charmes, but the best three cuvées, Les Varennes du Grand Clos (which has some sandstone), Clos du Chêne Vert (a warm spot), and Clos de la Dioterie (the oldest vineyard) have the most interest. The one to try first is Clos du Chêne Vert for an elegant balance that makes it more approachable. The white Clos de la Plante Martin is one of the finest white Chinons.

Domaine Frédéric Mabileau

FREDERIC
MABILEAU

LES ROUILLÈRES

ST NICOLAS DE BOURGUEIL

◉ 6 rue de Pressoir, 37140 Saint Nicolas de Bourgueil

📞 (33) 02 47 97 79 58

@ contact@fredericmabileau.com

💻 Frédéric Mabileau

🌐 www.fredericmabileau.com

◉ Saint Nicolas de Bourgueil

🍾 St. Nicolas de Bourgueil, Les Coutures

🧍 🏭 G N 🍷

28 ha; 175,000 bottles

There are at least ten producers with the name Mabileau in St. Nicolas de Bourgueil, but Frédéric Mabileau is by far the best known. The winery occupies small but workmanlike premises just by the main square in the center of St. Nicolas. The vineyards are mostly in St. Nicolas de Bourgueil, but there are some in Bourgueil. The domain started in 1988 with a 2 ha vineyard and then expanded up to 10 ha; Frédéric's father passed on another15 ha when he retired in 2003. There had been some disagreement: "My father had installed a harvester, there was a small confrontation; we wanted to express our cépage, our village, then the machine was definitively sold. By 2006, the harvest was all by hand." There are three cuvées from St. Nicolas: Les Rouillères (which comes from the original vineyard with the typical sandy-gravel soils of St. Nicolas) is vinified only in cuve with 5-10% carbonic maceration, and provides about 80% of production; Les Coutures comes from a mix of terroirs at the base of the slope, has no carbonic maturation, and is matured in a mix of old and new tonneaux; L'Eclipse, first made in 1996, and matured in new tonneaux, is produced only in the top years as an assemblage from old vines (50 to 60 years old) on calcareous terroir. In addition there is a Bourgueil from gravel terroir (Les Racines), an Anjou red (from parcels of Cabernet Franc just to the west of the appellation of St. Nicolas de Bourgueil), Chenin Blancs from Saumur and Anjou, a Cabernet Sauvignon from Anjou, and a rosé de Loire. Les Rouillères is ready to drink on release; the others require a couple of years. The usual style is fresh. "I want my wines to be representative of the appellation, giving off crisp fruit aromas, and easy to drink... we must have drinkability in St. Nicolas de Bourgueil," Frédéric says, but the wines become increasingly serious going from Les Coutures to Les Racines to Eclipse. The whites are more aromatic than I usually find with Chenin Blanc The estate bottlings are supplemented by a small negociant activity that is separate from the domain.

Domaine du Clos Naudin

14 Rue de la Croix Buisée, 37210 Vouvray

+33 2 47 52 71 46

leclosnaudin.foreau@orange.fr

Philippe Foreau

Vouvray

12 ha; 55,000 bottles

In spite of the shabby appearance of the buildings (just up the street from the much grander quarters of Domaine Huët), Clos Naudin has a good reputation for its sweet white wines. Dating from 1923, the domain has been run by Philippe Foreau since 1983. Located in the northeastern part of Vouvray, generally south-facing, the vineyards are almost entirely situated on perruches—clay soils with a high siliceous content—which makes the wines austere and closed when young. (Hermetic is the word used in French descriptions.) They are said to require a long time to open out into elegance. The domain is one of the most traditional in Vouvray. Fermentation occurs slowly in the cool cellars and usually lasts two months. There is no chaptalization. Malolactic fermentation is blocked. Wines are matured in 300 liter barriques, almost all old (a couple of new barrels are purchased each year out of the 100 total); they are concerned here to avoid the taste of wood. Production is 60% still wine and 40% sparkling wine. Sparkling wine comes in both nonvintage and vintage cuvées and is exclusively Méthode Champenoise (no pétillant). The division between dry and sweet wines depends on vintage conditions, but the domain is better known for its sweet wines. Made only in warmer vintages, these are characterized as demi-sec, moelleux, and the moelleux reserve. Visitors are nominally welcome, but reception is unreliable, so don't count on a visit.

Domaine François Pinon ★★

Vallée de Cousse, 55 rue Jean Jaurès, 37210 Vernou-sur-Brenne

📞 (33) 02 47 52 16 59

@ francois.pinon@wanadoo.fr

François Pinon

Vouvray

Vouvray Demi Sec, Trois Argiles

15 ha; 60,000 bottles

The winery appears a ramshackle affair, on the plateau above Vernou, just north of Vouvray, but the wines are among the most interesting of the appellation. We tasted outdoors in a lean-to porch, just off the winery, besides the family residence. François has forceful opinions about character and aging. "We have bought one or two parcels but the basic idea is to stay with our terroir and we've never tried to go beyond it," he says. There are 6-7 parcels now. When things go well there is a Pétillant and two dry cuvées (coming from clay and siliceous terroirs); sweet wines depend on vintage. Wines are named only by their terroir. On the Silex Noir with 14 g/l residual sugar, for example, the label makes no statement about sweetness. François think that to state demi-sec would give a false impression of sweetness. "The idea is to showcase the minerality of the terroir with a touch of sugar to add complexity." François shows a definite preference for developed flavors as he brings out older vintages back to the 1960s for tasting. The wines are deceptively straightforward when young—the dry wines show the minerality of the local terroir, the sweet wines tend to be more obvious—but wines with ten or twenty years of age show impressive development, yet always retaining freshness. The dry wines may be at their best after a decade, the sweet wines after perhaps twice that time. "My intention is to capture the flavors of Chenin, and as the wines become sweeter, that takes longer aging."

Domaine Olga Raffault

📍 1, rue-des-Caillis, 37420 Savigny-en-Véron

📞 (33) 02 47 58 42 16

@ infos@olga-raffault.com

🔲 Sylvie de la Vigerie

🌐 www.olga-raffault.com

🔘 Chinon

🚶 🏭 G N

25 ha; 100,000 bottles

Started by the eponymous Olga Raffault, who was still involved into the present century, the domain is run today by her grand daughter, Silvie de la Vigerie. The winery is a warehouse-like building in stone and wood, behind a courtyard a little off the beaten track. Vineyards are in the immediate vicinity, all the wines are Chinon AOP, and the grape varieties are exclusively Cabernet Franc and Chenin Blanc. The domain produces four red cuvées, one white, and a rosé. The focus is on the red cuvées, which come from different terroirs. Les Barnabés comes from young vines just by the winery, on sandy soils, and has no élevage. Les Peuilles comes from clay soils, and is matured in a mixture of tanks and wood. Les Picasses comes from calcareous soils, and has 14 months élevage in foudres. The domain describes it as a vin de garde, and in the past I have had many old vintages that matured well for around fifteen years. However, recent vintages of Les Picassses seem much lighter, and give the same faintly over-cropped impression of rather light fruits as Les Peuilles and Les Barnabés. I wonder if this is due to the introduction of Les Singulières in 2008, which is a selection of lots from Les Picasses: it is given longer maceration before fermentation and afterwards is matured for 24 months in barriques. Only small amounts are made each year, but perhaps their absence has deprived Les Picasses of its former quality. Although lighter in style, Les Singulières is the only wine of the domain today that recalls the character of the past. I quite like the white, which is a pleasant light wine for summer drinking.

Clos Roche Blanche

⊙ 19 route de Montrichard, 41110 Mareuil-sur-Cher

📞 (33) 02 54 75 17 03

@ closrocheblanche@wanadoo.fr

👤 Catherine Roussel & Didier Barrouilett

◉ Touraine

🍷 Touraine, Sauvignon

🚫 🋠 G 🍁

9 ha; 20,000 bottles

At the eastern edge of Touraine, vineyards were planted by the Roussel family at the end of the nineteenth century; the caves date from 1905. Catherine Roussel took over the domain in 1975, running it together with winemaker Didier Barrouillet. They started with conventional viticulture but converted to organic in 1992; they have tried biodynamic treatments but aren't convinced there's a significant difference. The size of the domain was reduced from its peak of 32 ha to 18 ha, which includes 12 ha of vineyards around the property (surrounded by woods, creating its own separate ecology), planted with Sauvignon Blanc, Chardonnay, Gamay, Pineau d'Aunis, and Malbec; other parcels in the adjoining villages are planted with Sauvignon Blanc, Cabernets Franc and Sauvignon, Gamay, and Malbec. Soils vary from clay to silex with a limestone subsoil. Production is half red and half white with just a little rosé (from Pineau d'Aunis). There is a small parcel of very old (115-year) Malbec vines, which are used to produce a monovarietal wine at yields that vary wildly from year to year. Most production is in stainless steel, the exception being the cuvée #5 of Sauvignon Blanc which is in old oak vats. The wines are bottled as AOP Touraine. There are six cuvées identified by varietal names, and three others. Cuvée Pif is a blend of 60% Malbec and 40% Cabernet Franc with tiny amounts of Cabernet Sauvignon and Pineau d'Aunis. Sadly the domain closed in 2015, but older vintages are still available.

Domaine de La Taille aux Loups *

DOMAINE
DE LA
TAILLE AUX LOUPS
2011
MONTLOUIS SUR LOIRE
LES DIX ARPENTS
Jacky Blot
Mis en bouteille à la propriété

8 rue-des-Aitres, 37270 Montlouis-sur-Loire

(33) 02 47 45 11 11

latailleauxloups@jackyblot.fr

Jacky Blot

www.jackyblot.fr

Montlouis

65 ha; 350,000 bottles

A wine broker at the time, Jacky Blot was regarded as a young Turk when he established Domaine de La Taille aux Loups by buying 7 ha in Montlouis in 1988. His attempts to introduce more precision into the wines were regarded with suspicion, but now he is regarded as a fixed feature of the appellation. Today he has 27 ha in Montlouis, divided among more than 30 parcels, and another 7 ha in Vouvray. Harvest is very extended at the domain, often lasting four or five weeks, as there is an attempt to harvest each parcel at a specific state of maturity. Young vines (less than twenty years of age) are used to make two sparkling wines, a Méthode Champenoise and the pétillant Triple Zero, which has no chaptalization, no dosage, and no liqueur de tirage. Virtually all the still wines, from older vines, are usually given extended maturation in wood, which has been a point of criticism. "I like long élevage in barriques or demi-muids and I hate the white Loire wines that have malolactic fermentation," describes the philosophy of the domain. There are five dry cuvées from Montlouis and three from Vouvray, distinguished by time of harvest, as well as by terroir and vine age, and a series of sweet wines from both appellations extending from demi-sec to liquoreux. In 2003 Jacky expanded into Bourgueil with the purchase of the 15 ha Domaine de la Butte, from which he produces four different cuvées. Visits are stated to be welcome, but visitors risk being ignored.

Sancerre

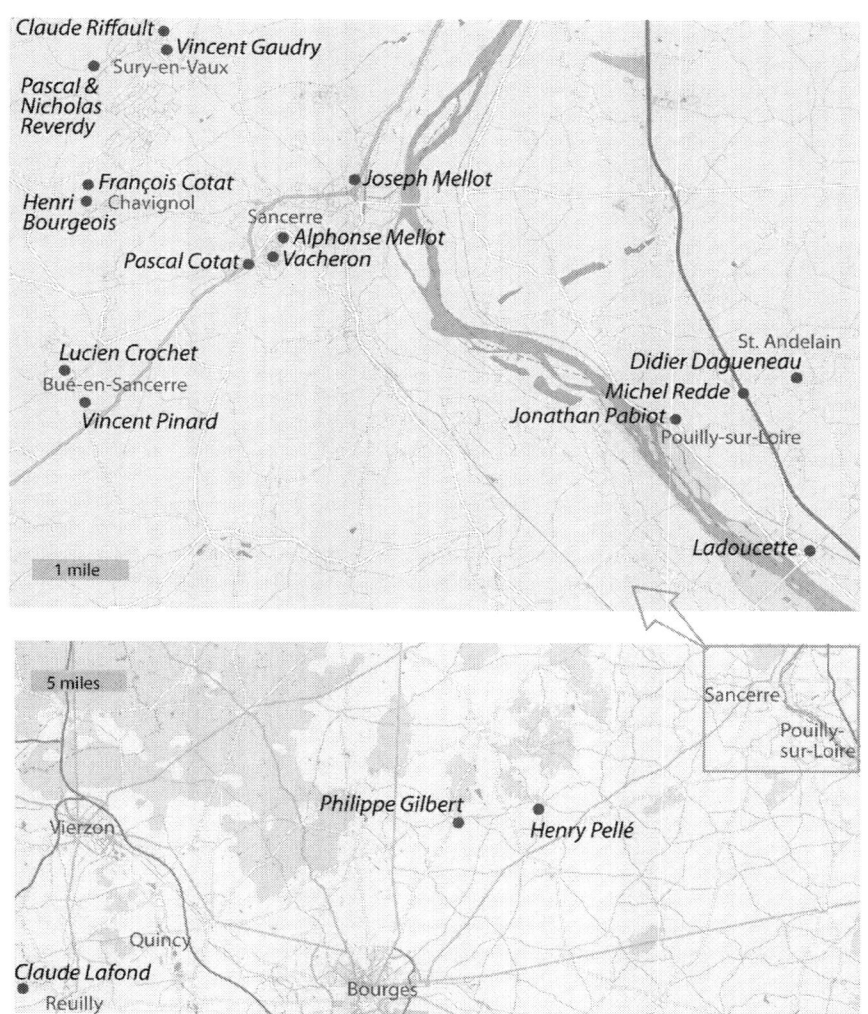

Claude Riffault
Vincent Gaudry
Sury-en-Vaux
Pascal &
Nicholas
Reverdy

François Cotat
Joseph Mellot
Henri Chavignol
Bourgeois Sancerre
Alphonse Mellot
Pascal Cotat Vacheron

St. Andelain
Lucien Crochet
Didier Dagueneau
Bué-en-Sancerre
Michel Redde
Vincent Pinard
Jonathan Pabiot
Pouilly-sur-Loire

Ladoucette

1 mile

5 miles

Sancerre

Pouilly-
sur-Loire

Philippe Gilbert
Vierzon
Henry Pellé

Quincy

Claude Lafond
Bourges
Reuilly

Domaine Henri Bourgeois **

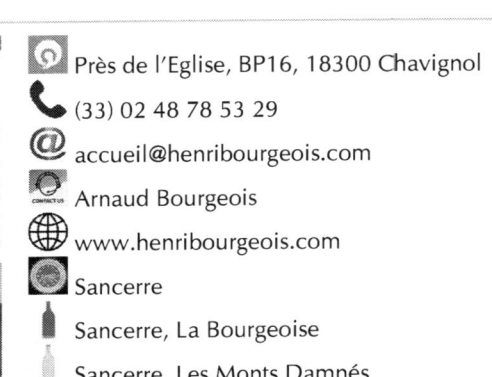

Près de l'Eglise, BP16, 18300 Chavignol

(33) 02 48 78 53 29

accueil@henribourgeois.com

Arnaud Bourgeois

www.henribourgeois.com

Sancerre

Sancerre, La Bourgeoise

Sancerre, Les Monts Damnés

74 ha; 600,000 bottles

One of the largest producers in Sancerre, this family-run domain occupies much of the village of Chavignol, with a hotel, restaurant, and tasting room; the modern gravity-feed winery is located at the edge of the town. Called by other vignerons half affectionately and half pejoratively "the American winery," it has a splendid view over the steeply rising vineyards. Spreading out from Chavignol, the domain has expanded steadily from its 2 ha in 1950. There are eight principal cuvées of white Sancerre, two from Pouilly, and wines from other appellations in the Centre. Going up the range, the cuvées represent distinct terroirs, mostly matured in a mix of stainless steel and old wood. The top cuvées represent individual plots: I especially like the elegance of Jadis from 40-year old vines in Monts Damnés, the subtlety of oak influence in d'Antan, and the completeness of Chapelle des Augustins from a unique plot of silex on calcareous subsoil. The range is impressive, all the way from quite traditional Sancerre with characteristic grassy notes, to wines from old vines at such ripeness that the flavor profile turns from citrus to stone fruits. Separate cuvées of Pinot Noir have been made since 1962: Les Baronnes and Les Bonnes Bouches are matured in a mixture of new and old oak, and the top cuvée, La Bourgeoise, comes from Vieilles Vignes (over 50 years old) and ages much like Burgundy. Bourgeois have also established Clos Henri in Marlborough, New Zealand, which is roughly equivalent in size.

Domaine François Cotat ✱✱

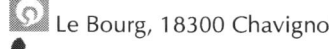

Le Bourg, 18300 Chavignol

(33) 02 48 54 21 27

sarlfrancoiscotat@bbox.fr

François Cotat

Sancerre

Sancerre, Cul de Beaujeu

4 ha; 30,000 bottles

The old Cotat domain, run by brothers Francis and Paul from 1947 to 1990, made powerful Sancerre in its own style, which is to say that late harvest sometimes produced wines with residual sugar. François Cotat inherited half of the domain in 1990, and has continued the policy of late harvest. Occasionally the wines have been judged atypical by the AOC. François remains in the old cellars, behind his house, right in the center of Chavignol. "I have no vines more than a kilometer away," he says. He inherited three small vineyards from the old Cotat domain: a hectare each in La Grande Côte, Les Monts Damnés, and Cul de Beaujeu (all Kimmeridgian terroir in Chavignol). He has since added another lieu-dit, Les Caillottes (made since 2005 as previously the wine was declassified because the vines were young). "Unfortunately, Sancerre today is technical wine, but me, I am not at all technical. I don't do anything—the least intervention possible. I am often the last to harvest, I look for full ripeness. I make vins de garde," he says, "They can be kept for up to twenty or thirty years, no problem. The wine is usually closed for the first five years and then begins to open." To make his point, he opens a 1995 Grande Côte that is still full of flavor. As a rule, Les Caillottes is the exception to drink relatively young, Monts Damnés is the most reserved, Cul de Beaujeu is more open, and Grande Côte is the fullest. The style is its own expression of Sauvignon Blanc typicity, and is always interesting.

Domaine Pascal Cotat ✱✱

Chemin des Groux, 18300 Sancerre

(33) 02 48 54 14 00

pascal.cotat@bbox.fr

Pascal Cotat

Sancerre

Sancerre, La Grande Côte

7 ha; 15,000 bottles

Brothers Francis and Paul Cotat established a domain in Chavignol in 1947. They shared production, bottling the same wines under their own separate labels. When they retired in 1990, they divided the domain between their sons, Pascal and François. (Part of the reason for the division was a regulation preventing independent producers from selling the same wine under two labels). Pascal makes his wine in new cellars in Sancerre. He got some of the oldest vines when the vineyards were split, and has two vineyards in Chavignol for Sauvignon Blanc production: a single hectare that is half of the Grande Côte lieu-dit (François owns the other half); and 1.5 ha in Les Monts Damnés. Both are on steep north-facing slopes, steep enough that all work has to be manual. Each vineyard makes a separate cuvée. The wine is fermented and matured in old demi-muids; coming from grapes harvested a week later than most in the appellation, it offers rich, full flavors, with significant aging potential. These are not wines to drink young, which would miss most of their complexity and distinction: they need time to develop full richness. They are unctuous without being fat, and rich but very fine, although alcohol can be high. A rosé comes from 4 ha in Sancerre. The 2010 rosé was declassified to Vin de Table because of an argument with the authorities (when Pascal refused to sell the town of Sancerre one of his vineyards to use as a parking lot, the vineyard was declassified).

Domaine Lucien Crochet **

LUCIEN CROCHET

2010

SANCERRE

APPELLATION SANCERRE CONTRÔLÉE
WHITE WINE

Le Chêne

MIS EN BOUTEILLE A LA PROPRIÉTÉ
LUCIEN CROCHET - 18300 BUÉ - FRANCE

Alc. 12% by Vol.   PRODUCT OF FRANCE   750 ml

Place de l'Eglise, 18300 Bué

(33) 02 48 54 08 10

contact@lucien-crochet.fr

Gilles Crochet

www.lucien-crochet.fr

Sancerre

Sancerre, Croix du Roy

Sancerre, Le Chêne

38 ha; 300,000 bottles

Created by Lucien Crochet from the vineyard holdings of his father and father-in-law, the domain is now run by Lucien's son, Gilles. Much larger than might be suggested by its modest exterior, the winery is a modern facility with sparkling new equipment in the center of Bué. Driving through his vineyards, Gilles points to nuances of terroir much as a vigneron might in Burgundy. The 90 individual vineyard parcels are all in the southern part of the appellation, around Bué, with 29 ha planted to Sauvignon Blanc on various terroirs, and 9 ha planted with Pinot Noir on Kimmeridgian terroir. The house style for whites develops from the mineral, citrus-driven Sancerre to the mélange of stone fruits and citrus in Le Chêne (from the Clos du Chêne Marchand), but the main difference between them is the greater delicacy and subtlety in Le Chêne. Moving from these wines, matured in stainless steel, to the single vineyard Cul de Beaujeu (introduced in 2009), the wine becomes rounder and riper, with more stone fruits than citrus; there is also the added factor of exposure to wood, with half new and half old. Only made in some years, from a plot of vines planted in 1956, the Cuvée Prestige offers a more evidently powerful fruit expression. In reds, the Croix du Roy Sancerre cuvée is a play on the name of Sancerre's famous Clos du Roy; and like its white counterpart, the Cuvée Prestige is made from old vines only in the best years. Its purity could easily come from Burgundy.

Domaine Didier Dagueneau ***

5 rue Ernesto Che Guevara, 58150 Saint Andelain

(33) 03 86 39 15 62

silex@wanadoo.fr

Charlotte Dagueneau

Pouilly Fumé

Pouilly Fumé, Pur Sang

12 ha; 50,000 bottles

The street address, 5 rue Ernesto Che Guevara, says a good deal about Didier Dagueneau, who created the domain in 1992 with only 3 ha. He rose to prominence as far and away the best (and most expensive) producer in Pouilly. The front office has a charming appearance, but the building just behind is a modern concrete, purpose-built, gravity-feed winery, designed by Didier to optimize wine production. Didier also started the Jardins des Babylone in Jurançon. After he was killed in a light aircraft crash in 2008, his son Benjamin took over as winemaker. The vineyards are in Pouilly except for a half hectare in Sancerre. "We make wines that are true, intended for keeping, they are meant to develop after time," is how Charlotte, Benjamin's sister, describes the style. Blanc Fumé de Pouilly is the only cuvée made by assemblage. Pur Sang comes from 2 ha of clay-flint, with very small pebbles, Buisson Renard comes from 1.5 ha of a thin layer of flint on top of clay, and the most famous, Silex, comes from deep flint at the parcel behind the winery. "It presents the longest potential for aging, but is also the wine that takes longest to develop," Charlotte says. Young vintages of all cuvées are restrained, but there is no mistaking the sheer purity of the underlying fruits: it's worth waiting five years for the full variety of flavors to develop. A mark of greatness is the increase of subtlety with age, with the 1996 Silex showing a delicate balance of truffles and fruits in 2014.

Domaine Vincent Gaudry

Petit Chambre, 18300 Sury en Vaux

(33) 02 48 79 49 25

Vincent Gaudry

www.vincent-gaudry.com

Sancerre

Sancerre, Vieilles Vignes

11 ha; 50,000 bottles

This small domain occupies an old building in the village of Sury-en-Vaux. They were bottling when I visited, and the portable bottling line had to be disassembled for us to descend to the cave below for the tasting. Started by Vincent's grandfather (as part of polyculture), the domain has many separate parcels today, and produces three white cuvées every year. Tournebride comes from the vineyard adjacent to the winery; Mélodie de Vieilles Vignes comes from 50-year old vines on clay-calcareous terroir; and Scorpion comes uniquely from silex terroir (the label just says Sancerre, but has an image of a scorpion, which is how Vincent refers to the cuvée). In some years another top cuvée, À Mi-Chemin, is made in tiny quantities (basically one barrel). Tournebride is vinified in stainless steel; the Vieilles Vignes in an equal mixture of stainless steel and wood; and Scorpion entirely in old wood. There's no fixed time for élevage. "I taste, like in the old times, and move it out of barriques into cuve when it tastes right," Vincent explains, but élevage is generally around twelve months. "Tournebride is usually good to drink after two years, the Vieilles Vignes and Scorpion, it's necessary to wait," he says. The house style is refined, elegant, and taut. Tournebride is quite accessible, but the linear purity of the young Vieilles Vignes and Scorpion really needs time to develop. The red is fresh and lively, and comes from a selection massale of the original Pinot Noir grown in Sancerre.

Domaine Philippe Gilbert

Route des Aix, 18510 Menetou-Salon

(33) 02 48 66 65 90

info@domainegilbert.fr

Philippe Gilbert

www.domainephilippegilbert.fr

Menetou-Salon

Menetou-Salon, Les Renardières

28 ha; 120,000 bottles

One of the larger properties in Menetou-Salon, the domain goes back to François Gilbert, an innkeeper who started making wine in 1768. Two generations ago, in 1959, Paul Gilbert was instrumental in creating the appellation. His son, Jean-Paul, actually reduced the size of the domain slightly; and the current Philippe Gilbert returned from a career in drama to take it over in 1998. At that time, it was two thirds Pinot Noir, due to the enthusiasm of Jean-Paul, who had studied in Burgundy. Today Philippe has increased the proportion of Sauvignon Blanc, and is aiming for an equal division between red and white. Vineyards on clay-limestone soils are scattered throughout the appellation in the villages of Menetou-Salon, Vignoux, Parassy, and Morogues. There are two cuvées of white and two of red. For each color, in addition to the domain wine there is the single vineyard, Les Renardières, (from a 4.7 ha plot divided equally between Sauvignon Blanc and Pinot Noir). There is also a rosé (from a plot of Pinot Noir that doesn't ripen so easily). "I am trying to prove that we have beautiful terroir in Menetou-Salon and we can mature wine for a long time. I want to represent the special elegance of Menetou-Salon; the wines are discrete but unfold slowly," says Philippe. The domain wines are elegant, offering a modern version of the traditional style, but the place to see the aging potential is Les Renardières, offering a ripe, textured expression of Sauvignon.

Domaine De Ladoucette

de **Ladoucette**
Pouilly-Fumé

APPELLATION POUILLY-FUMÉ CONTRÔLÉE

AC 12% 8940L   PRODUCT OF FRANCE   750 ML
MIS EN BOUTEILLE PAR de LADOUCETTE
AU CHÂTEAU DU NOZET, POUILLY-SUR-LOIRE (NIEVRE) FRANCE

Château du Nozet, 58150 Pouilly-sur-Loire

(33) 03 86 39 10 16

comte-lafond.de-ladoucette@orange.fr

Patrick de Ladoucette

www.deladoucette.fr

Pouilly Fumé

Pouilly Fumé

104 ha; 1,200,000 bottles

With 80 ha, La Ladoucette is one of the largest producers in Pouilly Fumé. Vineyards include all four soil types of the appellation, flint, sand, chalk, and clay; 90% are planted with Sauvignon Blanc. The youngest and oldest grapes are harvested by hand, the remainder by machine. Grapes are vinified separately from each parcel. The gravity-feed winery was built in 1990. Fermentation in temperature-controlled stainless steel tanks starts at 12 C and gradually increases to 22 C over 2-3 weeks. After fermentation the wine is matured for 18 months in glass-lined cement tanks (reflecting a belief that long term maturation in stainless steel would taint the wine with a taste from the steel). No oak is used. The major part of production is Pouilly Fumé. Baron L is a super-cuvée from selected lots in the best years: it has more intensity but also is more international in style. There are also two Sancerres, Comte Lafond which is blended from vines in 5 villages, and is fuller than La Poussie, which comes only from the eponymous village on clay and limestone soil. Both red and rosé are also made from the vineyards at La Poussie. La Ladoucette also owns the Marc Brédif domain in Vouvray, and Albert Pic and Regnard in Chablis. With its large scale of production, this may well be the public face of Pouilly Fumé for many: the standard is reliable if not remarkable. Recent vintages have shown a softening of the style and even a move towards more exotic fruits. The domain is not very receptive to visits.

Domaine Claude Lafond

Le Bois St Denis, 36260 Reuilly

(33) 02 54 49 22 17

claude.lafond@wanadoo.fr

Nathalie Lafond

www.claudelafond.com

Reuilly

Reuilly, Le Clos des Messieurs

40 ha; 300,000 bottles

Created by André Lafond in the 1960s with 2.5 ha that he inherited, the domain grew slowly to 6.5 ha. André's son Claude took over in 1977 and further expanded the domain. Today it is run by Claude's daughter, Nathalie. Owning 35 ha of the 200 ha planted in the appellation, this is the most important domain in Reuilly. There are also further vineyards in Valençay (just over the border in Touraine) and the IGP de Loire. The winery is a somewhat utilitarian modern building on the outskirts of Reuilly, built in 2012. Claude Lafond was instrumental in founding the Chai de Reuilly (which is adjacent and functions as a cooperative to make wines for vignerons to be released under their own labels), but since the new winery was constructed, the domain has been completely independent. Around 60% of production is white. The basic wines are matured in stainless steel, but a mix of stainless steel and barriques is used for the top cuvées. The style is relatively straightforward, with Sauvignon showing its grassy character, but cut by a touch of richness going up the scale as the wines spend longer on the lees and see more oak. The rosés are made from Pinot Gris rather than Pinot Noir. "We've always favored making a rosé from Pinot Gris because it's very delicate," says Nathalie Lafond. The reds tend to be a little tight, with a definite cool climate impression. The top cuvée in each color is called Cuvée André, after the founder. The wines offer a good illustration of the character of Reuilly.

Domaine Alphonse Mellot

◎ 3 et 6 rue Porte César, 18300 Sancerre

📞 (33) 02 48 54 07 41

@ alphonse@mellot.com

👤 Alphonse Mellot

🌐 www.mellot.com

◉ Sancerre

🍾 Sancerre, En Grand Champs

🍾 Sancerre, Les Romains

55 ha; 350,000 bottles

Alphonse Mellot occupies a rabbit warren of medieval cellars right under the town center of Sancerre, some dating from the fifteenth century (but modernized recently). Opposite is a modern building with the name of La Moussière, the main cuvée (about half of total). Vineyards in Sancerre include 30 ha in a single plot, and 13 ha of Pinot Noir, with more vineyards (Chardonnay and Pinot Noir) on the IGP Côtes de la Charité. Each cuvée of Sauvignon Blanc is distinct: La Moussière comes from a large block of Kimmeridgian terroir; La Demoiselle from silex; Satellite from Monts Damnés and Cul de Beaujeu in Chavignol (since 2008); Les Romains from a plot of 60-year old vines with flint on the surface and chalk underneath; Edmond comes from 40- to 90-year-old vines; and Generation XIX from 90-year old vines, at La Moussière. Each of the five separate cuvées of Pinot Noir is similarly based on separate parcels, with the top cuvées being En Grand Champs, a 1 ha parcel of 65-year-old vines at the top of La Moussière, and (50 m away) Generation XIX (named for 19 generations of Mellots) from even older vines. Both are true vins de garde. "The spicy quality with notes of fruit is the Sancerre typicity," the Mellots say of their reds. The house style is forceful: the steely roundness of the whites is what Chablis or the Côte d'Or might make of Sauvignon Blanc, and the reds can give the Côte de Nuits a run for its money. All are full of flavor, but always remain in balance.

Vignobles Joseph Mellot Père et Fils

SANCERRE
APPELLATION SANCERRE CONTRÔLÉE
LA CHATELLENIE
2008

Route de Ménétréol, 18300 Sancerre

(33) 02 48 78 54 54

josephmellot@josephmellot.com

Catherine Corbeau-Mellot

www.josephmellot.com

Sancerre

Pouilly Fumé, Domaine des Mariniers

115 ha; 2,000,000 bottles

The domain goes back five hundred years to César Mellot and has long been selling wine under its own name. "We are the sole domain to have vineyards in every appellation of the Centre," says Catherine Corbeau-Mellot, who has been in charge since the unexpected death of her husband Alexandre in 2005. All appellation wines come from estate vineyards, with half in Sancerre. Mellot also owns domains Pierre Duret and Jean-Michel Sorbe in Quincy that continue to be run separately. Grapes are purchased to make IGP wines. One of the largest producers in the region, accounting for almost 5% of all production, Joseph Mellot has its headquarters in a modern building constructed in 1990 just outside of Sancerre. "We need to represent the Joseph Mellot spirit, wine should be easy to drink, fresh and pure," is how oenologue Frédéric Jacquet describes the style. "You see terroir more clearly for Sauvignon Blanc with stainless steel," he says, explaining that most wines are vinified exclusively in cuve. More than three quarters of production is white. Except for a few cuvées matured in barrique, the emphasis is on fresh citrus fruits, increasing in intensity as the appellations change from Quincy or Reuilly to Sancerre or Pouilly Fumé. The wines are reliable representations of their appellations: I like the Pouilly Fumés best, with the Domaine des Mariniers and Le Troncsec illustrating the difference between assemblage and a single vineyard.

Domaine Jonathan Didier Pabiot

Pouilly Fumé

2012

Jonathan Didier Pabiot

⊙ 1 Rue Saint Vincent Loges, Pouilly-sur-Loire, 58150

📞 (33) 03 86 39 19 09

@ didier-pabiot@wanadoo.fr

Jonnathan Pabiot

Pouilly Fumé

Pouilly Fumé

19 ha; 90,000 bottles

This small domain is perched on the heights overlooking the river between Pouilly-sur-Loire and St. Andelain, occupying a small warehouse-like building next to the house. It's a very hands-on operation: Jonathan's wife, Nina, was running the labeling machine when I arrived. "We do everything in the same place," she says. Its history encapsulates change in the region. Didier Pabiot was making a single Pouilly Fumé that was sold in bulk or directly to the clientele. His son Jonathan wanted to try organic viticulture, so Didier gave him a hectare; later he bought a little more land, and started his own small domain. Then Didier decided to go organic after all, and in due course the two domains were joined back together. Yields have come down from 60 hl/ha to 40 hl/ha. The appellation wine is a blend of terroirs; Aubaine and Predilection are single vineyard wines from different calcareous terroirs. All three are vinified in stainless steel with minimal battonage. "Jonathan prefers the wine to take what it wants from the lees, not what we force it to take," explains Nina. Eurythmic comes from the same plot as Predilection but is matured in barrique. The labels of the cuvées say Artiste Vigneron, which is a fair description. House style is delicate and elegant, almost floral. Predilection is my favorite cuvée. The wines are restrained when young; to see full flavor potential, wait three or so years after release. The Pabiots were drinking 2006 and 2007 at home in 2014. The wines are a real bargain.

Domaine Henry Pellé

domaine Pellé
les bornés
menetou-salon
appellation menetou salon contrôlée

Route d'Aubinges, 18220 Morogues

(33) 02 48 64 42 48

info@henry-pelle.com

Anne Pellé

www.henry-pelle.com

Menetou-Salon

Menetou-Salon, Les Cris

Menetou-Salon, Les Blanchais

42 ha; 300,000 bottles

The domain dates from the start of the twentieth century. Three generations later, it was run by Eric Pellé until he died in an accident in 1995, when his wife Anne took over, aided by oenologist Julian Zernott (now in the Languedoc). Paul-Henry Pellé took charge in 2007. Most of Pellé's vineyards in Menetou-Salon are in the village of Morogues, where the 35 ha fall into 25 separate parcels. Another 8 ha are leased on long-term contracts. There are also 5 ha of Sancerre in the commune of Montigny. Production is two thirds white and a third red, with a small amount of rosé. The domain started in a small house across the street which is now used as an office; the modern production facilities were constructed in 1970 and extended in 1998. There are five white cuvées and five reds from Menetou Salon, each representing a single type of terroir, varying from flint to calcareous. "We try to work in Burgundy style, with each plot kept separate. We were the first in Menetou-Salon when my father started to do that in 1981," says Paul-Henry Pellé. Whites are fermented in stainless steel, and mature in varying combinations of stainless steel and wood. Reds are all aged in wood: Paul-Henry has backed off from extraction to go for more elegance, and has moved from barriques to larger 400 liter fûts; there is a little new oak. The style is elegant: whites show Sauvignon typicity in a fresh but round style; reds have precise fruits with good structure, and benefit from aging.

Domaine Vincent Pinard

Nuance

Sancerre

Vincent Pinard
vigneron

@ 42, Rue St Vincent, 18300 Bué

📞 (33) 02 48 54 33 89

@ vincent.pinard@wanadoo.fr

Cosette et Vincent Pinard

🌐 www.domaine-pinard.com

Sancerre

Sancerre, Charlouise

Sancerre, Grand Chemarin

17 ha; 100,000 bottles

"We are a very old family estate, winemakers for more than twenty genera-tions, established in Bué since the beginning," says Clément Pinard, who runs the domain today with his brother Florent. There's a modern cave under the family house, and a whole new winery behind for whites. There are 12.5 ha of Sauvignon Blanc and 4.5 ha of Pinot Noir. "The estate has increased in size but we have no plans to grow much more because we want to stay a family estate," Clément says. Vineyards fall into 40 different blocks in Bué: Sauvignon Blanc is planted on the chalkiest soils. Terroir is the driving factor in the white cuvées. Florès is a blend from various cal-careous parcels, Clémence from more clay. Nuance comes from 40-year-old vines on very chalky, stony soil. The three single vineyard cuvées are Petit Chemarin (from a late-ripening, west-facing site), Grand Chemarin (with southern exposure), and the famous Chêne Marchand. Harmonie was created in 1989 as an old vines Chêne Marchand with all new oak, but now has a quarter from other sites, and only 15% new oak. The Pinots are divided into the Sancerre from younger vines and the Charlouise from 45-year-old vines (with up to 70% new oak). In exceptional years there is a Vendanges Entières using whole bunches with no destemming. The sweet citrus fruits of the whites are delicate and fragrant, with increasing com-plexity in the single vineyards; the reds have precise fruits with silky smoothness.

Domaine Michel Redde et Fils

La Moynerie, RN7 La Route Bleue, 58150 Saint-Andelain

(33) 03 86 39 14 72

thierry-redde@michel-redde.com

Thierry Redde

www.michel-redde.com

Pouilly Fumé

Pouilly Fumé, Marjorum

41 ha; 240,000 bottles

Michel Redde wanted to be an artist, but started this domain in the hamlet of Les Berthiers. Today it occupies new quarters, built by his son Thierry in 2001, just on the other side of the autoroute. Thierry's son, Sébastien is in charge of the cave, while his brother manages the vineyards. Michel's paintings hang on the wall of the tasting room, which is guarded by an elderly Labrador named Sauvignon. The wines almost all come from Pouilly Fumé, with six cuvées, each representing an assemblage from the same terroirs or a single vineyard, although the domain also maintains 1.5 ha of Chasselas for two cuvées in the Pouilly-sur-Loire appellation. All wines are vinified in the same way, in a mix of foudres and demi-muids, in order to allow terroir to be the sole determining difference. They spend 12 months in wood followed by a year in cuve before release. Although I admire the objective in preserving the old varieties, I'm not entirely sure I find enough flavor interest in the Chasselas. The Sauvignons from Pouilly Fumé all show a very understated style when young, with a faintly citrus character: they tend to be more interesting on nose than palate, which might indicate promise for the future. The revelation at the domain, however, was a tasting of older wines, when the 1996 Pouilly-sur-Loire Cuvée Gustave Daudin put in a creditable performance, and the La Moynerie cuvée of the same vintage from Pouilly Fumé seemed much younger than its age.

Domaine Pascal & Nicolas Reverdy

Maimbray, 18300 Sury-en-Vaux France

(33) 02 48 79 37 31

reverdypn@wanadoo.fr

Pascal et Sophie Reverdy

Sancerre

Sancerre, Les Anges Lots

14 ha; 90,000 bottles

Pascal Reverdy took over this family domain in 1985, and moved completely into estate bottling. His younger brother Nicolas joined him in 1993, and after his accidental death in 2007, his wife Sophie came into the domain. The winery has some old, workmanlike buildings in the hamlet of Maimbray. Pascal makes the wine, from 10 ha of Sauvignon Blanc and 4 ha of Pinot Noir. The introductory cuvée in red, white, and rosé is called Terre de Maimbray, as the vineyards are all in the coteaux above Maimbray, on very steep slopes of Kimmeridgian terroir (with inclines of 30-40%, rising up to the plateau at around 300 m elevation at the top). The white Terre de Maimbray is vinified in stainless steel, with six months' élevage on the lees. An old vines cuvée, Les Anges Lots, from vines more than sixty years old, is matured in a large wooden cuve with battonage for ten months. It's richer than the Terre de Maimbray, with stone fruits adding to the citrus, and a sense of restrained power. The red Terre de Maimbray is matured in a mixture of barriques and larger barrels of old wood; it's intended to be a vin de plaisir. Cuvée Nicolas comes from the only vineyard parcel that's not in Maimbray, a plot of pure calcareous terroir in Bué; matured in demi-muids with about one third new, it's intended to be a vin de garde, and shows good purity of fruits with an earthy, mineral, character. The rosé is fresh and savory, made in the tradition of white wine.

Domaine Claude Riffault

SANCERRE
LES CHASSEIGNES
CLAUDE RIFFAULT

Maison Sallé, 18300 Sury en Vaux

(33) 02 48 79 38 22

claude.riffault@wanadoo.fr

Stéphane Riffault

www.clauderiffault.com

Sancerre

Sancerre, Les Chasseignes

13 ha; 80,000 bottles

The Riffault family was in polyculture involving cereals, goats, and a few vines until viticulture became increasingly important during the fifties. Stéphane Riffault has been making the wine since 2001, in a modern cuverie, constructed twenty years ago, in the hamlet of Sury-en-Vaux. Vineyards are in the northern part of the Sancerre appellation, with about fifty parcels altogether. Each area is vinified separately to make a cuvée representing a specific terroir. "We've always separated the lieu-dits," Stéphane explains. There are five white cuvées; four come from calcareous terroir, with varying amounts of clay and fossil deposits; and one (Les Chailloux) comes from a siliceous plot at the eastern edge of the appellation. Les Boucauds and Les Chasseignes are vinified in a mix of stainless steel and barrels; they have relatively short élevage, and represent half and a quarter of production, respectively. Coming from smaller areas, Les Denisottes, Les Chailloux, and Les Desmalets are vinified entirely in wood, with élevage lasting around nine months. Stéphane favors 500 liter barrels. The style of the whites is towards precision and clarity of fruits, often subtle and understated when young, except for Les Desmalets, which is more forceful. There's a little red from Les Chailloux; and both red and rosé come from a single 2.5 ha vineyard on Kimmeridgian terroir, La Noue. The rosé usually comes from the younger vines. The red La Noue tends to be quite tight on release and needs a couple of years to soften.

Domaine Vacheron **

1, rue du Puits Poulton, 18300 Sancerre

(33) 02 48 54 09 93

vacheron.sa@wanadoo.fr

Jean-Laurent Vacheron

Sancerre

Sancerre, Belle Dame

Sancerre, Le Paradis

50 ha; 250,000 bottles

Located in the center of Sancerre, with old cellars running under the town, Domaine Vacheron is run by cousins Jean-Dominique and Jean-Laurent. The domain wine comes from an assemblage of all their terroirs, but since the first single vineyard wine, Les Romains, was introduced in 1997, they have been moving towards expression of individual terroirs. Jean Laurent's view is that this depends on getting the vigor and the date of harvest right. "At middle vigor you get citrus flavors, which give the most complexity. The window of harvest for Sauvignon Blanc is just four days for each block: you have to be in that time if you want to display varietal character," he says. Les Romains comes from silex; Guigne-Chèvres, Chambrates, and Le Paradis come from different calcareous terroirs. There are also reds from all terroirs, including Belle Dame from silex; its refined character makes you think of Volnay. The house style here is towards precision and elegance in the whites. The same sense of refinement and purity shows for the reds. Both whites and reds from silex show a quality of taut tension; those from calcareous terroirs are broader, but still have that delicate blend of citrus and stone fruits. Both reds and whites age unusually well: top vintages of reds are good for twenty years; and a 1983 appellation Sancerre white was lively and savory in 2014 (quite developed, of course, but with the restrained style offering subtlety). There's a distinctive view of varietal typicity here.

Index of Estates by Rating

Index of Estates by Name

INTELLIGENT GUIDES TO WINES & TOP VINEYARDS

WINES OF FRANCE SERIES

1 Bordeaux

2 Southwest France

3 Burgundy: Chablis & Côte d'Or

4 Southern Burgundy, Beaujolais & Jura

5 Champagne

6 Alsace

7 The Loire

8 The Rhône

9 Languedoc

10 Provence and Corsica

WINE OF EUROPE SERIES

11 Barolo & Barbaresco

12 Tuscany (coming soon)

13 Port & the Douro

NEW WORLD WINE SERIES

14 Napa Valley & Sonoma

BOOKS by Benjamin Lewin MW

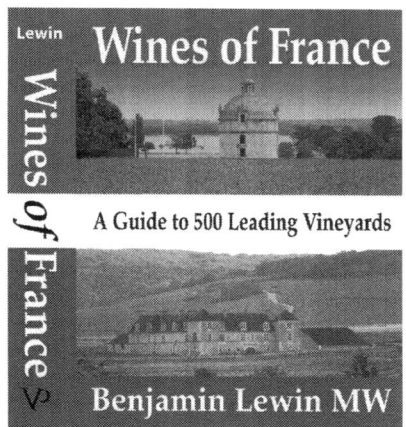

Wines of France

This comprehensive account of the vineyards and wines of France today is extensively illustrated with photographs and maps of each wine-producing area. Leading vineyards and winemakers are profiled in detail, with suggestions for wines to try and vineyards to visit.

Claret & Cabs:

the Story of Cabernet Sauvignon

This worldwide survey of Cabernet Sauvignon and its blends extends from Bordeaux through the New World, defines the character of the wine from each region, and profiles leading producers.

In Search of Pinot Noir

Pinot Noir is a uniquely challenging grape with an unrivalled ability to reflect the character of the site where it grows. This world wide survey of everywhere Pinot Noir is grown extends from Burgundy to the New World, and profiles leading producers.

Wine Myths and Reality

Extensively illustrated with photographs, maps, and charts, this behind-the-scenes view of winemaking reveals the truth about what goes into a bottle of wine. Its approachable and entertaining style immediately engages the reader in the wine universe.

What Price Bordeaux?

A revolution is underway in Bordeaux. Top chateaux have been obtaining unprecedented prices for their wines, while smaller chateaux are going bankrupt. Extending from the changing character of Bordeaux wines to market forces, this unique overview reveals the forces making Bordeaux wine what it is today.

About the Author

Benjamin Lewin MW brings a unique combination of qualifications in wine and science to bear on the world of wine. He is one of only 300 Masters of Wine, and was the founding Editor of Cell journal. His previous books received worldwide critical acclaim for their innovative approach. Lewin also writes the myths and realities column in the World of Fine Wine, and contributes to Decanter magazine, Wine & Spirits, among others. His blog on wine is at www.lewinonwine.com. He divides his time between the eastern United States and the wine-growing regions of Europe, and is presently working on his next book.

61737602R00087

Made in the USA
Lexington, KY
18 March 2017